STUDIES   7

Already published in the series:

HARDY:
THE MAYOR OF
CASTERBRIDGE

by

DOUGLAS BROWN

EDWARD ARNOLD

First published 1962
by Edward Arnold (Publishers) Ltd
25 Hill Street, London W1X 8LL

Reprinted 1964, 1966, 1970, 1973, 1976

Cloth edition: ISBN 0 7131 5064 5
Paper edition: ISBN 0 7131 5065 3

For Keith Barry and other Colleagues

'I wanted him to say one word about his writing before we left and could only ask which of his books he would have chosen if, like me, he had had to choose one to read in the train. I had taken *The Mayor of Casterbridge*. "And did it hold your interest?" he asked.'

VIRGINIA WOOLF, in
A Writer's Diary

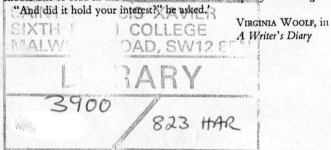

Printed in Great Britain by
The Camelot Press Ltd, Southampton

General Preface

The object of this series is to provide studies of individual novels, plays and groups of poems and essays which are known to be widely read by students. The emphasis is on clarification and evaluation; biographical and historical facts, while they may be discussed when they throw light on particular elements in a writer's work, are generally subordinated to critical discussion. What kind of work is this? What exactly goes on here? How good is this work, and why? These are the questions that each writer will try to answer.

It should be emphasized that these studies are written on the assumption that the reader has already read carefully the work discussed. The objective is not to enable students to deliver opinions about works they have not read, nor is it to provide ready-made ideas to be applied to works that have been read. In one sense all critical interpretation can be regarded as foisting opinions on readers, but to accept this is to deny the advantages of any sort of critical discussion directed at students or indeed at anybody else. The aim of these studies is to provide what Coleridge called in another context 'aids to reflection' about the works discussed. The interpretations are offered as suggestive rather than as definitive, in the hope of stimulating the reader into developing further his own insights. This is after all the function of all critical discourse among sensible people.

DAVID DAICHES

Acknowledgements

The Author wishes to acknowledge the kind permission given by Macmillan and Co. Ltd. and the Trustees of the Hardy Estate to quote from *The Mayor of Casterbridge* and other novels of Thomas Hardy; by Longmans, Green and Co. Ltd. to quote from his book *Thomas Hardy*; and by Mr. Leonard Woolf to quote from Virginia Woolf: *A Writer's Diary*.

Contents

1. A Rehearsal of Themes

The labourer in Weydon countryside

It reads like some grotesque old country legend, this brief, disquieting drama of a wife-auction. But Hardy was quick to advise the sceptical that such transactions did indeed take place, and within living memory: one, near Dorchester itself. The memory serves him in two ways. First, it originates his saga of mid-century Dorchester in the earlier decades of the nineteenth century. It has the effect of drawing together the twenties, the forties and the eighties: for the eighties were the years of composition. They provide the vantage-point. Second, in a grim fashion, it treats of primary human relationships under the arbitration of the cash nexus. It subordinates the human to the mercenary. In a violent image it puts a quiet and hopeless woman up for auction; and her price climbs by guineas, guineas whose paper and coin can be heard clinking and crackling.

The novel is about transition. It charts the change and disorder in the southern English communities, that accompanied the disturbance of agriculture in the national economy. It explores a related disordering of human values, the consequence of new forms of commerce, and of the attitudes these forms promoted. Its general tenor reflects, too, the pressure of powerful economic forces, perceptible in their effect but not understood. All these Hardy's imaginative art explores, not conclusively but taking the feel. There is something of stern confrontation; something of bewildered withdrawal. There is an effort to bear faithful record. These are the predicaments, this is how life goes, for societies taking the strain of change.

From the start, it is human society that engages Hardy's imagination rather than the individual consciousness. Here are wayfarers: a family approaches a village. The light alters: a labourer, fit and skilled, seeks his proper work. We know Henchard first in his agricultural and social rôle, by his clothes and his tools. He comes before us less as a human being than as a representative: 'His measured, springless walk was the walk of the skilled countryman,' and the stern and swarthy aspect, the dogged and cynical indifference, reveal themselves in the step of the foot and the movement of clothes. And in this spirit the interests of a portrait artist seem to be at work. We see Henchard's wife bright and warm in sunlight and apathetic in shade. (Hardy's comment on her quiet apathy seems portentous; but it puts before us, in 'nature' and 'civilization', two terms useful for understanding the changes disturbing the local societies of the south.) The relationship of husband and wife has staled, through the difficulties of his livelihood. But the countryside feels lively about them, and the wayfarers approach the village with 'sundry distant shouts and rattles' in their ears, a token of community; and they meet, as its representative, another labourer with his tools.

Weydon-Priors offers neither work nor home. And the dogged hopelessness implicit in the situation of migratory labour sounds eloquently through the first voices to be heard. 'Pulling down is more the nater of Weydon. There were five houses cleared away last year, and three this; and the volk nowhere to go—no, not so much as a thatched hurdle; that's the way o' Weydon-Priors.' A tension develops between the gay distant shouts, and the hopelessness here. It's Fair Day: the first of a succession of festivities that punctuate Hardy's novel, reminders and enactments of an older and continuing reserve of local tradition and pleasure in commonalty. Hardy is striking out the kind of equipoise his novel needs, between the residual vigour of the older community and the necessities of change. The Furmity Woman's tent harbours a warm, tenebrous, protective fellowship; and the novelist's absorbed prose records a responsive warmth of allegiance.

There is real fellow-feeling here, there is an unforced community of interests; and there is the numbed marriage relationship, and the sleeping child. The talk turns to the obstructions of agricultural labour, and Hardy subtly mingles with the tones of Henchard who wants to be free and worth a thousand pounds, the sound of an auctioneer's voice in the field outside selling old horses. The voices inside and outside, all the detail of village life, seem to verify the grotesque transaction that impends. Mercenary forces, and that irrational, merely competitive desire of acquisition to which the auctioneer's technique addresses itself, are securing control. The patience and unease and regret of the quiet wife, and the growing insecurity of the men and women around her, lodge in the mind. The late swallow, momentarily trapped and bewildered, and seeking release from an unnatural environment, fixes the attention and deepens it. (We half-remember this swallow in the caged goldfinch of the closing pages.) Then the auction begins. There is an odd implicit tribute to what remains priceless, in the dream-like inversion of the usual procedure. The price goes up and up, without bidders. And Susan Henchard bows her head 'with absolute indifference'.

This patient impotence of the country victim is a constant image in Hardy. Here, it is the plight of the travellers on the first page, now wrought to a higher pitch. Financial exchanges circulate about Susan of which she is innocent and which she cannot engage. So, in due course, it is to be for the mayor in the larger community. The sailor who enters at the crucial moment is another wayfarer; by his very calling a man of no continuing city. Though the body of the novel locates itself securely in a place and a time—Dorchester, the forties—yet exiles, travellers, the homeless, move through its pages, perpetual reminders of what the new commerce and the new techniques are doing to older social stabilities. 'Where do the sailor live?' asks a voice out of the shadows. 'Seafaring natures be very good shelter for shorn lambs, and the man do seem to have plenty of money,' says another, curiously bringing together three important images of the novel. And here all comes to a point of focus.

> The sailor hesitated a moment, looked anew at the woman, came in, unfolded five crisp pieces of paper, and threw them down upon the table-cloth. They were Bank-of-England notes for five pounds. Upon the face of this he chinked down the shillings severally—one, two, three, four, five.
>
> The sight of real money in full amount . . . had a great effect upon the spectators. Their eyes became riveted upon the faces of the chief actors, and then upon the notes as they lay, weighted by the shillings, on the table . . .
>
> . . . With the demand and response of real cash, the jovial frivolity of the scene departed. A lurid colour seemed to fill the tent, and change the aspect of all therein.

It is a concentration of the whole novel's movement; an embryonic vision. A moment later Henchard's vexed 'She'd no business to take the maid—'tis my maid,' hints at the tendency to treat relationships as an extension of the self, of its properties. And Susan Henchard's obedient acquiescence, loyally to be sustained through years to come, reflects her credence in purchase power and in society's complicity in that power. Now darkness falls, and the community melts away from the hay-trusser; the Furmity Woman disappears and the last candle is extinguished.

The rehearsal of themes is still incomplete, even with that ebbing away. There is also the movement from candle-extinction to sun streaming through crevices. The freshness of morning, new life stirring and old life resuming after misery, or death, or defeat: the ordinate vitality of the sun—here is another recurring theme. Tinkling of sheep-bells, nesting of yellowhammers, heavily dewed grass under the newly-risen sun, accompany a bracing of the personality as Henchard does what can be done to make amends. Natural rhythms and personal rhythms meet. Even the stillness here falls into place in a rhythm of labour. But renovation in the context of such an act as Henchard's, in this old legend (as it seems), can only take the form of shouldering consequences, making the gesture of reparation, and dourly 'going on'. He is again the hay-trusser, a representative figure, as he approaches the altar rails. He makes his vow there, where village piety has its social traditions, because there has been a grievous offence against the sanctities and stabilities of the older community, a kind of rupture. It is again a wayfarer who sees 'a thick jet of wood smoke suddenly start up from the red chimney of a cottage near', and who later disappears into Casterbridge.

The morning scene seems, too, to clear the mists of the pages before; to sharpen our sense of the ordinary Weydon-Priors; to carry an illusion of nearer time. I have concentrated upon the deposits of imagery that this remarkable narrative leaves behind because these can delicately guide the reading of the saga that now unfolds. But the sombre conviction of that narrative is itself imposing. This is what the past feels like to the concerned, imaginative participant. It has been brought to life, yet it has kept its distance, its aura. Hardy is communicating a sense of its momentum, its processes; not, particularly, a sense of the human heart. He is faithful to that, but he does not illuminate it.

2. 'Things Fall Apart'

The mayor in Casterbridge town

We are in the eighteen-forties, the decade of Hardy's boyhood; shortly we are to enter Dorchester, where (during those years) he had formed his deepest impressions and commitments. To this very town, the Caster-bridge of his novel, Hardy had himself returned, drawn back to Dorset-shire from the London world; had built himself a house and settled permanently. He ranked by now among our more eminent novelists. After a long period of anxiety and bad health he had recovered vigour and confidence. Although (for financial reasons) he had serial publication in view, he worked at *The Mayor* for over a year and completed the whole to his design, before publishing the first instalment. His mind and imagination were testing out the boyhood time. But he, and those among whom he lived, knew what had happened since and what was happening still. The past was not simply the past.

As the novel moves into the forties, the image of wayfarers troubles the mind again. Mother and daughter approach the village and the fair, walking 'with joined hands . . . the act of simple affection'. They see how the years have told. The fair registers 'mechanical improvements' but its real business has dwindled. 'The new periodical great markets of neighbouring towns were beginning to interfere seriously with the trade carried on here for centuries.' Here is the impact upon stable and accustomed communities of forces outside, and we can see why Hardy locates his saga in a market town. Mother and daughter 'thread the crowd' and the old Furmity Woman's lament suggests the poignant incapacity of the tight-knit local societies to withstand the shocks of change. They simply disintegrate. She herself is to reappear among the human derelicts that these inexorable and useful processes have discarded, in Casterbridge's Mixen Lane. She 'opens the sluices of her heart' to speak her elegy, and a vital part of Hardy's imagination resides in this sense of loss. It is the first of a series of elegiac passages that stud the novel as do the scenes of communal mirth. And the Furmity Woman's last words engage plainly the evolution of the novel itself: 'But Lord's my life—the world's no memory: straightforward dealings don't bring profit—'tis the sly and the underhand that get on in these times!' So the new economy is felt to bear upon the old community.

But through the daughter the new generation makes its voice heard in a disconcerting way. 'Don't speak to her—it isn't respectable . . . Mother, do let's go on—it was hardly respectable for you to buy refreshments there. I see none but the lowest do.' Caste-feelings to that effect had no part in the Furmity Woman's tent twenty years back (her lament makes clear). Elizabeth-Jane aspires to withdraw into her own segment of the new community. It's a fragmentation, true, that continues from the earlier divisions by trade and skill; but those divisions hadn't this fracturing effect. Hardy here starts to explore a facet of the processes of change his world has to come to terms with: something bewildering, something Elizabeth-Jane herself, once in Casterbridge, and more fully sensitive, recoils from. In the meantime she, the younger, appears the guardian of Respectability; she remains guardian throughout the journey into Casterbridge, the first sojourn there.

Susan Henchard's sale was the first, the plight of the Furmity Woman is the second image of the predicament Hardy seeks to bring to legendary force and clarity in Henchard himself: representatives of an older style of living and working, dependent upon an earlier economy; involved in new processes whose authority they cannot comprehend nor hold back; broken and defeated. Nor ought there to be any holding back; but the distress of their predicament remains, and the possibility of real loss. What ought to happen? Hardy intimates a way through the maze in the pages that discuss Elizabeth-Jane's rearing.

. . How zealously and constantly the young mind . . . was struggling for enlargement; and yet now, in her eighteenth year, it still remained but little unfolded. The desire—sober and repressed—of Elizabeth-Jane's heart was indeed to see, to hear, and to understand. How could she become a woman of wider knowledge, higher repute—'better', as she termed it . . .

Hardy's imagination is always probing here; he knew this area of difficult confinement so well in himself. So Clym Yeobright determines; Grace Melbury and Edred Fitzpiers are joined by the same desire; it is Jude's story. How to come to terms with a world in which this had to happen to the enclosed agricultural communities? Hardy himself, in private life, was studying contemporary philosophy systematically and deeply, in the effort to make terms of his own with an inharmonious experience. From this point in the novel, as the two wayfarers approach the City and migration is over (until catastrophe is complete) the Elizabeth-Jane who seeks to comprehend becomes a guiding consciousness. The situation in Casterbridge, in all its complexity, impacts particularly upon her; her response is, as it were, barometrical. She is like Waverley or another protagonist in Scott engaging related processes of change. For her desire of advancement, knowledge, new opportunities to extend the possibilities of living, command our allegiance too. This has to be set alongside the Furmity Woman's lament. A balance is being struck.

THE OLD COUNTRY TOWN

In a sense the whole novel so far has been a pilgrimage to Casterbridge. When the two women ascend the last hill they contemplate the City—a hint of Jude's meditations about the distant Christminster. What does this City *mean*? Sounds of distant revelry (as from the fair at Weydon) permeate the reflections. 'An old-fashioned place': so it strikes the trained forward movement of the girl's consciousness. And Hardy hints a sense that his readers must find it so too, forty years after; a few inhabiting another Dorchester, most inhabiting quite another England. We find an imagination of the civil centre of an agricultural community, inextricable from surrounding villages and arable landscape. Here and there is a sentence of mere opinion; Hardy intrudes. But for most of these three vital pages the art takes care of itself. Dwellings and streets have grace and order, trees enfold variety of houses in their own variety of kinds, there are no suburbs, and avenues lead out into cornfields. The community seems at once protectively fortified, and sheltered; and bold in coppery sunlight. All is mosaic. By a fine stroke of art, twilight and lamplight come as the women enter; as though a shadow falls across all this interweaving and ordered variety: defensive now, a little shuttered. 'The lamplights now glimmered through the engirdling trees, conveying a sense of great snugness and comfort inside.' Things become nearer and more distinct. Sharp footnotes remind us of demolitions and alterations since those days, and we recognize that we are in the realms of imaginative sociology, that a whole style of life is latent in the wayfarers' vision. The paragraph of the gaze into the shop windows takes that word 'mosaic', with its suggestion of interlocking variety, right into trade and occupation. Material and historical detail inform a nostalgic imagination.

The sociological blends with the fabular [1] in a way peculiar to Hardy's fiction. We may say that the memoried vision of a boy has been set to work by the deep attachments of a man, but that is not all. The eyes are wide open. It is still a subtle art that ends this vision with the ringing of old curfew and the clatter of shutters falling (the first communal activity Casterbridge visits upon the reader). Here, in this City of Agriculture, is the novel's field of change; to whatever extent humanly valid and satisfying, processes set in motion outside are at work here, and the novel is to explore and hold in balance the consequences.

Deft humour informs the imagination, too. For it really is a delicately humorous art that sharpens its hold upon time and change by listening to the clocks and bells in the way it does, watches the women devouring the loaf of bread, and so leads from what may have seemed idyllic, legendary, vision into such distinctness of time and place and voice; into issues of sound bread and sound beer. The brass band and the illuminated festive building collide with—

> 'Oh, 'tis the corn-factor—he's the man that our millers and bakers all deal with, and he has sold 'em growed wheat, which they didn't know was growed, so they *say*, till the dough ran all over the ovens like quicksilver . . . I've been a wife and I've been a mother, and I never see such unprincipled bread in Casterbridge as this before.—But you must be a real stranger here not to know what's made all the poor volk's insides plim like blowed bladders this week?'

Hardy doesn't often invest his country voices fully with dialect; when he does, a particular local vigour pushes through, as here. The human invades the Casterbridge idyll all right; and the interlocking of human and mercenary and agricultural interests is there triumphantly in the angry clash of terms—*unprincipled bread*. The festive band plays 'The Roast Beef of Old England', and if the humour is obvious it is also purposeful. Neither old England nor her roast beef make valid currency in these streets now. The trade in wheat suffers perturbation, and the corn-factor, willy nilly, must play his part. So the movement as a whole from the first vision of the town to the bitter voices and the band does not point clearly in one direction or another; it veers about.

[1] Here, and elsewhere in this study, I use 'fabular' in the strict sense of 'having the quality of fable'.

MAYOR AND COMMONALTY

We take the feel of Casterbridge before we meet its mayor. And from now on rarely half a dozen pages pass without some occurrence bringing the business of the town back into the texture. The figure of the mayor takes its force and confidence partly from the sustaining civic rôle. He bodies the Casterbridge of the forties into personal terms. We meet him presiding at civic festival; gazing with the two women into the King's Arms we seem to experience the Furmity Tent writ large. The whole community participates in this mirth, and windows are open so that their representatives at feast can be supported by the invisible poor. The sense of community is the more vivid for our consciousness of two isolated spirits cut off from common life, and their vision invests the scene again with the curiously fabular quality Hardy's art sustains so confidently. And of course the appearance of Henchard in this transformed guise *is* fabular, a fairy-tale transformation, echoing old country ballads and anecdotes. From skilled labourer migrant in the country to corn-factor and mayor in the country town—he is still the essentially *representative* protagonist. And Hardy contrives not a new portrait but a reminder and extension of the old. The corduroy-clad labourer with his established place in society has become the mayor ('What a gentleman he is! and how his diamond studs shine!') wearing the clothes of an office which sorts uneasily with the older vocation, whose heavy gold chain and old-fashioned evening suit suggests compromises with another milieu. We seem to see a portrait; and the novelist reflects as one might upon the character a portrait suggests. 'Rather coarse than compact', 'rich complexion which verged on swarthiness', 'flashing black eye', 'an occasional almost oppressive generosity'—it would be a mistake to confuse the art that gives us this psychology with the subtlety of a George Eliot's. The strength in the characterization of Henchard rests in a kind of confidence, learned through general observation and serious reflective habits trained by traditional country experience and wisdom. And it rests in a quality of distance and reserve such as belong to older styles of story-telling; not so much creative sympathy, imaginative out-going, as respectful disengagement, even from the pivotal figure: and a consequent clarity and certitude. With changing forms of social life Hardy is an imaginative explorer; with human nature and human behaviour he is the confident delineator, wary, astute, but not profound.

But the admixture of social connivances into the hay-trusser's new rôle is another matter. Susan watches and thinks of past days and 'shrinks back'; Elizabeth-Jane feels elation at discovering herself 'akin to a coach'. It is still part fairy-tale for them. But status, affluence, economic power, starting out of 'dealings in wheat, barley, oats, hay-roots and such like' and as if by invisible pushes growing beyond these, are real here. The dinner is ordered so as to reflect degrees of status, and outside the voices of the commonalty appraise their mayor as the merchant and employer who has 'risen' by his dealings. Yet the sense of power is illusory. When the rude shout interrupts the formalities and the question of responsibility for unprincipled bread comes up, we feel the stunned incapacity of the old-style factor (for all the clothes of office) in contemporary mercantile transaction. 'I was taken in in buying it as much as the bakers who bought it o' me.' Hardy deposits another sharp image along the way: the victim of 'the market', of unchecked economic relationships, through whom others too have to suffer. There is a feeling of strength (Henchard has it here), there are gestures of amelioration. But the sources of weakness pass uncomprehended.

THE YOUNG COMPETITOR

The talk of labourers outside the King's Arms lent substance to Henchard's rôle. Now a further gathering of distinct classes of Caster-bridge society prepares the entry of Farfrae the Scot. He too impinges on the tale like a legendary figure (though his smart travelling bag fixes him in the contemporary scene). He has the magic knowledge of the Other World—that's how his new techniques are felt here. He is the Canny Scot of tradition; he is the Stranger from Far Away (especially in the Inn later). Yet he is part of the history of Hardy's own decade too: a pointed reflection of something important in the farming tragedies of the times. Records show how frequently Scots farmers did come south and save farms and little communities from bankruptcy and collapse, by new and thrifty, wary, adaptable methods.[1] Farfrae is at once a saga figure and a part of the history of Dorset: the same blend as Henchard himself, who receives the magic formula, and reassumes the responsibilities of the Corn Distributor as the festivities decline. A grim facetious humour peels off the social veneers of the banqueters, the daytime poses ordained by social forms (as Hardy notes). A more natural, less dignified and paraded human solidarity comes in.

[1] I owe the point to Miss R. Young, the social historian.

Farfrae enquires for a respectable hotel, and the two women, following him, pursue respectability too. Elizabeth-Jane still sees him in heroic style; a 'golden haze' enfolds him yet later, after the singing in the inn parlour. The move from the King's Arms to the Three Mariners is also a further entry into the traditional past: an Elizabethan building (now demolished) frequented by its own clan of vocations and local figures; its architecture registering survival into an uncongenial present, its fittings beyond local restoration. The twelve bushel strength of home-brewed ale remains; and after the business of the corrupted wheat, this tells. Past and present lodge together here. This old ale house is frequently before us as a place in contemporary Casterbridge where issues of respectability and appearance are vital. Elizabeth-Jane's service of Farfrae sends uneasy tremors out into the story.

Farfrae's identity for the saga fills out when the rivals come together. He is another migrant—more entirely so. He is the picaresque hero seeking his fortune—but 'in the great wheat-growing areas of the west'. And with that he enters yet closer into the history of those times. Emigration reflected the contemporary agricultural collapse, while it was the impact of farming the vast virgin lands out west that so fatally damaged English farming. His going suggests there is no place in the old enclosed southern communities even for the new skills and energies that might preserve by transforming. 'New processes for curing bad corn', the techniques Farfrae brings with him, belong at once to the folk ballad world of John Barleycorn, and to the facts and anxieties of Hardy's times. The instinctive generosity with which the migrant offers the corn-factor his new knowledge matters too. (It is rather too facile to read this novel with a notion of Farfrae as the disingenuous sharp-wit.) Henchard reveals less admirable habits of mind, preoccupied with public estimate of his 'credit'. He can't see Farfrae except in a trading relationship, he must buy the information. But the new technique is offered as response to another's need; and Henchard eventually unlocks his heart, warming to the Scotsman's generosity and individuality. The context (at first) is still 'usefulness to his business'. Then comes the refreshing feel of natural friendship—though Hardy's discriminating phrase is 'Henchard's *warm* conviction of his *value*'. There is warmth, but also a sharp sense of value —the value of 'judgment and knowledge', of the scientific skill Henchard knows he lacks, and without which 'strength and bustle' cannot stabilize agriculture in contemporary Dorsetshire. Farfrae's reluctance is important. The bringing together of these men marks a stage in the saga;

B

a temporary stability may follow. But Hardy's imagination deals with the forties from the vantage-point of nearly half a century on. Farfrae, like Jude, wants to see the world, he wants to break right out. Within its compass, our story envisages a Farfrae who stays, and who assumes Henchard's inheritance. But here, at this point, the art offers its darker hint that—given the inheritance—Farfrae too must suffer displacement in the end.

Carefully studied, this scene between the two men exhibits that fine, creative impartiality which really nourishes Hardy's art. It springs from his wary commitment to the good of his society. The balance he strikes comes of a valuable disquiet; he knows that the continuance of Caster-bridge depends upon a process of painful accommodation, human as well as technical. Obscurely, he knows too that it must depend upon securing real control, real responsibility: not the mimic responsibility of mayoral robes, and feasts which the poor may watch through windows, and 'market faces'; not passive submission ot bewildering economic pressures while play-acting an emotional and spiritual master-fulness which but obscures Casterbridge and its countryside from its mayor, and him from his community.

That both home, and exile from home to see the world, have their place, is one theme of the next scene too. After the mayor in his com-munity we watch the emigrant Scot build fellowship about his strange-ness. The novel adds a third festive occasion, its music even more significant. It's Elizabeth-Jane ('fresh from the seclusion of a sea-side cottage') who observes and feels the varied, compact society of the inn. But the episode of the Scots song is not easy to respond to. True, there is a characteristic broad irony in the singing of the love of home by a voluntary exile; Coney lurches into Farfrae's poise with the thrust of dialect. Yet the scene before is still fresh in memory. We know that the real preservation of home depends upon some measure of freedom from it, upon adventuring forth. Without that, the disintegration already widespread in agricultural societies can only increase. Whose, then, is the real loyalty? The sophisticated, tender singing—something given freely in answer to request, not without its genuineness—is to echo through the novel. Then again, balancing it, the room and the men have bulky 'solidity of specification' (in James's phrase) as against the hame that is melodized with a dying fall. Or they have until Hardy seems to apply too much pressure, and a facetious note overplays the vulnerable provinciality here. What distinguishes Farfrae by the end of the scene is an element of seriousness (touched with self-dramatization) that speaks for maturity, the consciousness of decisions to be made. But Hardy delicately puts a doubt to that in turn; Elizabeth-Jane builds her fantasy around him, sees him partly as a way of escape from provincial inadequacies, partly in snob terms—'respectable and educated'. We may baulk, by now, at the first; but the second sticks.

CASTERBRIDGE BY DAYLIGHT

Now Henchard is to be joined both to that quiet image of the past, his wife Susan; and to Farfrae, the alert, vital migrant farmer whose skills and education have in their keeping whatever future may be. Chapter IX is one of Hardy's gayest and most skilful. It connects the adjustments in human relationship with a fuller apprehension of Casterbridge. The further analysis of the market town, in the mellow air of imminent autumn, stands between the near-parting and eventual union of the men; again between these comes Susan's decision and her daughter's shy advance. We may distinguish opinion from art in this description of Casterbridge[1] but the rather pontifical or facetious offers to interpret or explain are perfectly natural to the civic actuality. I mean such things as the touch that opens the chapter, or the statement about complementary life quickened into irrefutable art when bees and butterflies from the cornfields wing their way down the High Street; or the supple delicacy of this:

> And in autumn airy spheres of thistledown floated into the same street, lodged upon the shop fronts, blew into drains; and innumerable tawny and yellow leaves skimmed along the pavement, and stole through people's doorways into their passages with a hesitating scratch on the floor, like the skirts of timid visitors.

In this Casterbridge Henchard is 'habited no longer as a great personage but as a thriving man of business'. And Susan's appreciation of his essential warmth loses itself in the procession of wagons 'loaded with hay up to the bedroom windows. They came in from the country . . .' They are his wagons, and they finally impel Susan to him. The Casterbridge that Elizabeth-Jane sees has open doors of private houses, the strong colours of autumn flowers blazing vividly against the crusted stonework

[1] Hardy is here a writer who cares about country values, reaching out uncertainly, even clumsily, towards a complacent and sophisticated urban reading public: he can't find the right manner of address.

of years. The town feels not only the 'pole, focus, or nerve-knot' of sur-rounding country life but also a steady growth out of the Roman past. We take the reality of traffic and exchange between town and fields in the overflow of animal, vegetable and harvesting life onto pavements, into houses. Even the rain floats 'like meal' in Casterbridge, and continually through the novel sun and rain (especially sun) the natural sources of growth, replenishment, harvest, tell out their vigour and refreshment. One of the main streets is Corn Street; and the usual transactions of business have the quality of human contact, expressing itself—to clumsy extreme—in the gesture of the whole personality backing the deal. Casterbridge itself seems to suggest that wholeness of personality. All is reciprocal here—in trade, in the joys and troubles of men. Hardy makes no large claim for this society's stability or resources; his art speaks only with measured reasonableness. But it is art we have here, not just social history, nor an idyllic City; by its selections and identifications the imagination sharpens our sense of civic welfare. These are pages for attentive study. The novel does not bear its title for nothing, it really is about Casterbridge and its protagonist is identified as Casterbridge's First Citizen (as we say nowadays). In history, Casterbridge was passing in the forties, was gone yet further by the eighties. But what renovation is possible? is necessary? What ought most to be cherished during the processes of change?—Such are the questions the pages ask of us.

Elizabeth-Jane's first sight of Henchard's yard, its hay barns and granaries and high storehouse, her surprised sight of Farfrae 'in the act of pouring some grains of wheat from one hand into the other', solidify this older Casterbridge. And Hardy's backflash, now, to the moment of union between the two men has added force. It is as though the abund-ance and naturalness of the old town informs Henchard's warmth and forthrightness, 'fierce in its strength'; whose affection and need, together with the Dorsetshire countryside, draw Farfrae to him. 'He looked over the fertile country that stretched beneath them, then backward along the shaded walk reaching to the top of the town.' They agree; and 'Now you are my friend . . . Let's clinch it at once by clear terms.' The clear terms wed the outside of the story the more firmly to its undersea forces and tensions. Then follows the striking of the balance. The same analysis of Casterbridge stands behind the treatment of Jopp, the first consequence of Henchard's impulsive appointment. He acts coarsely, insensitively, unjustly. There's no instinct of relationship here, no sense of reciprocal responsibilities within the commonalty or between master and man.

Henchard is found wanting. The first sign of the autocrat, we may say; or is it a latent aspect of old Casterbridge—a too great reliance upon human nature, too little upon rights legally secured—suddenly developed to danger-point? In terms of the plot Hardy's imagination is cunningly inventing to reproduce his deeper pattern, this hasty failure in responsibility is to show itself a self-destructive force. That, in part, is Jopp's rôle: a stage villain at times, yet earning his place in the imaginative pattern.

There is one more imagination of Casterbridge to follow, and again it is so woven into the texture as to divide Henchard's meeting with Elizabeth-Jane from his reunion with Susan. At the opening of XI we discover more clearly the relationship of Casterbridge with a much remoter past: 'Casterbridge announced old Rome in every street, alley and precinct.' This continuing presence of the oldest times, we know, peculiarly fascinated Hardy; but he makes his private preoccupations imaginatively meaningful. True, the prose is encumbered and pompous (like the celebrated 'set piece' on Egdon in *The Return of the Native*) but at later points in the novel—the opening of XIII for instance—art replaces opinion, and we experience the strange connections of an avenue overshadowing a Roman wall, an evening sun shining deep yellow to penetrate the sycamores, and steep dwellings in radiance; while you look out beneath these same sycamores upon the tumuli and earth-forts of the distant uplands. Does the insistence upon Roman Caster-bridge pull the drift of the novel a little off-course? Towards a merely aesthetic Past? Perhaps. But along with it goes a strong feeling for growth, slow change, necessary process, history. And that informs the entire saga of the defeat of the mayor of Casterbridge.

CHANGING RELATIONSHIPS

From this point the tale moves along currents and cross-currents of human feeling and human relationship and becomes more continuously a story of men and women. We begin with the 'gentle delicacy of manner' of Henchard's treatment of Elizabeth-Jane, conscience and the sense of obligation once roused. But Hardy locates the delicate relationship in a dining room oppressively dark with weighty symbols of civic affluence. When Henchard begins his confession to Farfrae, again the listener's eye travels over these absurd and ugly objects. There is a discrepancy between the man and the world he has levered himself into; his seems a severely compromised strength. Not surprisingly ('As mayor, with a reputation to keep up . . .' 'You must start genteel . . .') his consideration for his kin has regard also to his public image. A shadow from the outer world has already fallen across Casterbridge; before its economy takes the force of world trade, the submarine shapes of metropolitan social forms intrude to trouble human relationships and natural dignities and domesticities. A difficult play of motives is upon the man with 'dark pupils which always seemed to have a red spark of light in them', when genuine compunction, and a flinching away from the shabby-genteel old-fashioned clothes his daughter wears, and the set habit of resolving all issues (including painful human ones) into commercial equivalences, together lead him to send the five guineas that shall buy back the wife he sold. The gesture only repeats the offence; yet it is also a tacit gesture of repentance. And how poignant is the meeting between husband and wife when it comes; Hardy's compassion, his 'purity of feeling' [1] allow no falsity. It happens deep in the shadow of the Past, in the Roman arena: which recollects the obvious thing about their reunion, but also insinuates a deeper truth, one sustained by the narrative: an image of Susan as the representative of an older, simpler order of country life in all its vulnerable courage and dependence. Her husband, however, means to establish her with due regard for respectability and position, and plans a public ceremony, the marriage of mayor with lady.

The growing relationship with Farfrae has its eloquence too. His perspicacity is a clue to his being, and so is his care in finance; the warm unwelcome Henchard who intrudes upon him shuts Farfrae's account books with friendly force. He has warmth of his own: the ardour, the romantic glow in which he first appeared, speak for his inner buoyancy. But he has more grace, tact, alertness. Henchard's impulsive confession to him begins in a sense of oddness 'that a relationship starting in a business ground' should so swiftly take in most personal issues. The novel stands by the insight that the human, the mercenary, and the labouring are intact parts of a man; you can't separate the human calibre from the rest. The confession scene is a violent image for this perception; and its substance reminds us sharply that with Hardy, as with Dickens, some of the invention for these magazine instalments of Victorian fiction is corny stuff. The energy of narrative imagination carries us past, often buoying up shoddy material by the strength of the underlying conception; absurd projections have deep solid strata beneath. But we need not be

[1] Middleton Murry's phrase, in an essay on Hardy in *Aspects of Literature*.

deceived about the material itself: so with the matter of Jersey in *The Mayor*; and the returns of the dead or the forgotten to trouble the living.

Human relationships develop alloyed with respectability and concern for public appearance. Mother and daughter are 'installed, with a white-aproned servant and all complete'—and an astringency in the style suggests Hardy's alertness. Henchard's wife looks at him 'and his dress as a man of affluence, and at the furniture he had provided for the room—ornate and lavish to her eyes'. How much of fear and self-mistrust, how much of vanity, in this sustaining of his rôle? we want to ask. The reported gossip leans the same way: 'The masterful and coercive mayor of the town was captured and enervated by the genteel widow, Mrs. Newson.' With Susan's 'entry into her husband's large house and respectable social orbit', into a house where 'the two unassuming women scarcely made a perceptible addition to the contents', with a husband 'as kind to her as a man, mayor and churchwarden could possibly be'—with these, a tissue of respectabilities concludes. And the tart Dickensian prose of that last tribute warns us of the way the public figure is supplanting the man.

Yet when they are wedded one lovely touch is sufficient to remind us who, really, these are, how they belong to Casterbridge: 'It was a windless morning of warm November rain, which floated down like meal, and lay in a powdery form on the nap of hats and coats'—that, and the ensuing talk of workmen outside the church. For here the talk is superbly managed, reflecting status and poverty and a man's worth in cash and the related social decorum, in a flow of sharp, wise perceptions. In the earlier scene of the Three Mariners, Hardy's purposes with his countrymen obscure his art; here, his imagination honours them and moves easily in its natural channels. The occasional Shakespearean mannerism is a flaw; the rare false note is easy to detect: but we should not miss the many true. The wedding itself consecrates a past relationship here, and there is a fiery vitality about the elegiac passages built round it. The talk thrives upon detailed memory, it is laced with proverbial phraseology; stylized, certainly: but in such a way as to enact, rather than exclude, fine stamina—a marvellous gaiety works through the anecdotes of Mrs. Cuxsom's mother.

Hardy goes on, as ever, to adjust the balance between the old and the new. One aspect of Henchard's thriving business and social prestige is the lure to a false decorum, dissociated from old Casterbridge; but the new ease and abundance mean for Elizabeth-Jane opportunities of growth in mind and personality. Hardy's way of thinking about her may be cumbrous, but the perceptions tell. Yet the social forms exert their meaner pressures too. Her reasonableness about dress can't prevent her projecting an unreal personality into the civic milieu. We know it by the sunshade—the implicit withdrawal that so delicately conveys: the newly sensitive skin protected from strong light and warmth (and the source of the cornlands' fertility). Sunshades are fashionable, no new dress is complete without one to match. So she must adapt herself as Henchard does to the forms required by wealth and position in the changing world. The originating force of these forms—the new metropolitan city—is to become clearer when Lucetta appears. The mayor's increasing snobbery about his daughter fuses with his appreciation of her utility as a token of Conspicuous Consumption.[1] But Hardy subtly indicates her unwillingness to become this person and her dependence upon traditional provincial experience.

And Casterbridge takes her to itself—the Casterbridge of this menaced and transitional moment between two worlds. The notation is tart and elegant—at XV for example. Hardy knows just what he is about. 'As soon as Casterbridge thought her artful it thought her worth notice.' When a new fashionable outfit has been purchased, sunshade and all, 'the whole structure was at last complete'. (It is a moment to recall when Lucetta creates herself a personality from a choice of London dress fashions.) There is Elizabeth-Jane, Henchard's daughter and soon Farfrae's young lady, whom Casterbridge makes what it can of. There is also the girl who watches and feels the course of the tale. Hers is the high room that looks down into granaries and hay stores; hers the 'quiet eye' that discerns Henchard's increasing dependence upon Farfrae's capacities, that watches the new techniques of ledger and letter supplant the old, that questions the human gains and losses. She regards the precarious dominance and the demandingness of the one, the more detached mental alertness of the other—Henchard's 'second pair of eyes'. Impetuous cordiality, and genial modesty, distinguish the one from the other: and the geniality suggests a serenity and self-possession, as well as a warmth answering to the more turbulent energies of the mayor.

So the tensions separating them reveal themselves first in regard to personal relations. The story of Whittle is true village anecdote—the voices, the extravagances. And it throws sharply out (just before the

[1] Veblen's *Theory of the Leisure Class* is a most useful companion to this, as to so many, Victorian novels.

disruption of an alliance which has made the merchant's corn and hay traffic thrive as never before) the most important issue of all: which side does the more real humanity rest with? Farfrae's response to Whittle's humiliation—is it instinctive sympathy? or offended propriety? or a latent flair for labour relations? Henchard's bullying anger—is it offensively inhumane? or a fierce and troubled aspect of some deeper quality of relationship with others? ('During the day Farfrae learnt from the men that Henchard had kept Abel's old mother in coals and snuff all the previous winter.') Hardy holds the scales trembling and even; more so, during Henchard's gloomy discovery of his fall in reputation. There is delicacy as well as acuteness in Farfrae's understanding of the older man, yet the doubt about the depth of his response remains. He stops his song with a self-rebuke at the house of the bereaved, at once sensitive, and decorous—primarily which? But in the next chapter Henchard's are the gestures and courtesies that are well bred, mechanical. With characteristic aplomb Hardy uses the community at festival to clarify the changing relationships, pull the two further apart, and precipitate the crisis. The prose continues to hold the balances trembling, and its terms go on colliding in pointed ways. There is 'the pressure of mechanized friendship' in Henchard's customary arm upon the young man's shoulder, there is the vexed, brilliant phrase about the improvements to any plan of his own for festivity that Farfrae would be sure to suggest 'in his damned luminous way'. There are the two festive entertainments; one flamboyantly generous, a prodigal display: yet it ends (however dismally as festival) with a quiet distribution to the poor and hungry—paternalist, perhaps. The other, brilliantly devised as commerce, and advertised, is for fee; but it incorporates (what the bitter mayor looks in to find) a wild Highland fling, dancing, music, unforced gaiety.

THE RUPTURE

Out of the concealing darkness Henchard prefers to sights and sounds like that, come country voices recalling home truths, summing up the processes of change.

His accounts were like bramblewood when Mr. Farfrae came. He used to reckon his sacks by chalk strokes all in a row like garden palings, measure his ricks by stretching with his arms, weigh his trusses by a lift, judge his hay by a chaw, and settle the price with a curse. But now this accomplished young man does it all by ciphering and mensuration.

It is the danger of being 'honeycombed clean out of all the character and standing that he's built up in these eighteen year' that prompts the final rupture. With whatever else, the older order nourishes an ego-centred paternalism, and to preserve that public image Henchard lurches into folly. When he hears of Farfrae's competitive response to dismissal, his furious outburst is very revealing—but in no creditable way. No issues are settled, the balances continue to tremble between the old Casterbridge and the new. Then he engages the proffered competition—'a tussle at fair buying and selling, mind'; his confidence rests in his 'amazing energy', in the 'unruly volcanic stuff beneath the rind' of the self. But in the town council there prevails a foreboding sense that energy has had its day. Henchard 'walks down the street alone'. Financial intrigue is alien to his energy; and much as he desires human property, bearing his name before the public like his wagons and granaries,[1] a family to extend his repute, yet he will not intrigue in human relations either. The strategy of securing Farfrae as a son-in-law he repudiates.

Farfrae has his generosity and high ethical code too. He won't take custom from his patron. (Or is there, too, the astute cultivation of the right reputation?) 'He was once my friend. I cannot hurt the trade of a man who was kind to me.' Hardy's colliding terms are still subtle: 'unprincipled bread'—'hurt the trade'. And there is energy to match energy, 'northern energy' it is called. 'His northern energy was an over-mastering force among the easy-going Wessex worthies.' (In that last phrase don't we feel mere opinion tilting the balance? Or should we remember, rather, the difficult public Hardy designs to take with him?) The northern energy has the luck of trade with it, too; and luck, like the veerings of weather, tends in Hardy's art to reproduce those undis-tinguished vaster forces actually at work upon this and all other agri-cultural enclaves: economic pressures that regard no local needs and ties, that serve new industrial centres of power.

As the tension gathers, the novel revitalizes Casterbridge itself, and extends Elizabeth-Jane's participation. The effect is to underpin the changing human relationships with the real presence of the civic and agricultural facts and situations they body forth. 'Wheatricks overhung the old Roman street and thrust their eaves against the church tower', barns and houses alternate, town and fields stand adjacent, and the sounds of two distinct worlds mingle naturally together. Equally, the very old,

[1] See chapter XIV.

the old and the modern interlock, and social forms have shaped themselves from the mosaic. 'A street of farmer's homesteads—a street ruled by a mayor and corporation, yet echoing with the thump of the flail, the flutter of the winnowing-fan, and the purr of the milk into pails . . .'—Hardy is concerned both to bring a community's order to bear upon his protagonists, and to imagine truthfully a civic milieu that can reflect, contain and reciprocate the rural. It is perhaps a dream; but coolly, humorously dreamed, and for a purpose of clarification.

One strand remains to this part of the novel: the affection between Elizabeth-Jane and Farfrae. It starts in the beautiful scene of accidental meeting—another stretch of village anecdote, if you like, but done with rare art. Elizabeth-Jane retreats to the loft while her assigned lover waits below. 'A winnowing machine stood close beside her, and to relieve her suspense she gently moved the handle; whereupon a cloud of wheat husks flew out into her face, and covered her clothes and bonnet, and stuck into the fur of her victorine.' It's as though her instinctive affiliation is disclosed for us. The wheat-husk covered girl looks forward to Giles Winterborne immersed in his apple-tree awaiting Grace, or covered in pips from cider-brewing; or the reddleman of *The Return*. With what delicacy this 'husks and dust on you' becomes the occasion of the human contact (Farfrae blows them off). The balances seem to tremble again. Is the alien merchant-economist blowing away the chaff that makes her a simple country girl? But then he steps out of the legendary rôle, as it were, and becomes warm, ingenuous, candid about the singer and the song. We realize that the 'irony' of the first Three Mariners scene did not quite encompass this reflective and intelligent spirit.

SUSAN HENCHARD'S DEATH

It is imaginative art that sounds the elegiac note just now, when Henchard's commitment to strife is firm. His wife's death signals the passing of some *virtu* from the old order (for she has most purely reflected its passive, suffering strength). The follies into which he stumbles, as if impelled towards his own defeat and conspiring with its instruments, also have an aura of death about them. Separated from the council, separated from the festivities, he is 'a gloomy being' who 'wanders away from the crowd'. The community whose buoyancy he rode supports him no more; it is moving with the times. And separated, Henchard's strength is disabled, it feeds upon an image of the public self since it cannot take sustenance from a real rôle. So Hardy suggests one aspect of coming defeat; suggests, too, how fiery energy turned in upon itself becomes extreme, and connives at doom.[1] Into 'mortal commercial combat' the mayor (fast in his rectitudes) drives the young merchant—responsibility seems his. It is 'a war of prices' too. Hardy's terms keep the vaster areas of his century's history in mind. He strikes his balance in a new phrase, 'Northron insight matched against Southron doggedness', a sharper focus upon the conflict. The older communities, moving with national and continental tides, have only doggedness to offer. It is the quality of the defeated Clym Yeobright (blind, but for a small circuit of vision: a working area of furze) and of the defeated Tess at Flintcomb Ash. And insight? Luminous reason, mercantile astuteness, might salvage the life of these communities, soften the severities of social change and human loss. Yet (for Hardy) insight has no ending, it moves into gloom. 'Perfect insight into the conditions of existence' is not life-enhancing. Happiness finds her last stay upon earth where insight is longest postponed.[2]

As we approach Susan Henchard's death, her husband's behaviour in Casterbridge deteriorates; 'gazing stormfully past' his rival, he creates absurd fantasies about their relationship. New areas of the past disclose themselves—Lucetta's letter, Susan's letter. While Elizabeth-Jane watches by her dying mother the clock ticks until time's passing becomes a resonant clang. The prose is gentle, sharp. But we need only remember how George Eliot would create such a scene (how she would reflect in her own voice, and how her creatures in their unique privacies would reflect) to see the limits of Hardy's art. The mind here is the novelist's own, and his 'subtle-souled girl' is but a vague projection. But the death itself, what is common to all, Hardy relates admirably, and as a social reality. Farfrae hears of it first: he too must confront the image of transience. Then it is the talk of the town pump, authentic voices turning over the details of custom and domestic convention, and voicing a lament which is buoyant with an inner rhythm of continuity. Here is an art able to give a voice to 'humanity', and only Scott at his greatest can match, in its kind, the end of XVIII. And with what blithe subtlety the very notion of continuity takes on market terms: 'Why should death rob life o' fourpence?'; and again, how gently extensive and representative Susan's living ways become in the final requiescat: 'Well, poor soul; she's helpless to hinder that or anything now,' answered Mother Cuxsom.

[1] See Section 3 of this study.
[2] See *The Dorsetshire Labourer*, or pp. 39-42 of my *Thomas Hardy*.

'And all her shining keys will be took from her, and her cupboards opened; and little things a' didn't wish seen, anybody will see; and her wishes and ways will all be as nothing!' Her burial place, we find later (when it suits Hardy's art to note it) is with Roman mothers in a place of long continuous sepulture.

STRATEGIES FOR SECURITY

Now some intuition seems to suggest that only a powerful amassing of possessions can enable continuance of the older ways: an incompetent venture towards that structure of empires of financial power that drive the new communities, at whose mercy lies the mimic market of Caster-bridge. As Henchard aspires anew to the possession, and labelling, of Elizabeth-Jane (and shortly after, to the marketing of her) the pre-tentious furniture looms forward again. The imagination is here (it seems) almost painfully alert to the significance of the human relationships. The prose registers the old man's vibrating mind compassionately, reveals the emerging need for natural relationship smothered by the urgent drive to obtain possession. Mercantile subtlety and human ten-derness mix in the strategy of his engagement of his daughter to him. '"I don't want you to come to me all of a sudden," said Henchard in jerks, and moving like a great tree in wind.' His legendary signification is in the simile: and it is the same giant figure who opens his wife's sensitive letter, learns a yet harder truth about the past, and 'regarded the paper as if it were a window-pane through which he saw for miles. His lips twitched, and he seemed to compress his frame, as if to bear better.' When Elizabeth-Jane comes to him, the 'blaze of satisfaction' is warmed by his passionate self-regard; yet 'tenderness softened it'. But the feeling of possession chills: 'Elizabeth was his at last . . . He was the kind of man to whom some human object for pouring out his heat upon . . . was almost a necessity.' What, then, is Henchard establishing in his household? As often Hardy's art seems rather to question than to illuminate; its mood is provisional.

For as the story unfolds it seems that Henchard cannot build stable relationships about himself as mayor or as merchant. The manipulation of Elizabeth-Jane is already dust and ashes for him by the end of XIX. His very nature moves against relationship: it is a truth about the arrogant passionate man in the story, but it is also a truth about Casterbridge's First Citizen, about the saga hero. Stable family relationships, a firm and simple moral bond backing them, were a strong element in older agricultural and provincial life[1] and in Henchard's suffering we feel it disintegrate. Hence, perhaps, the louring darkness of the scenes of his loneliness in this part of the novel; the darkness or twilight of the scenes turning upon his paternity. The prosperous merchant, the figurehead mayor, sets about making Elizabeth-Jane a not-herself, an emblem of status in the changing public world. She for her part is moving in another direction. She has sloughed off the respectability she so earnestly desired at first; or, having secured a modicum of security asks no more. She desires none of the fashion and prestige he wills for her. She seeks maturity through study (as her creator did), reading diligently and long: like Clym, and Fitzpiers, and Jude. This possible other response to the tragic plight of provincial life is never long lost sight of in *The Mayor*.

Henchard's demands upon her show a failure of real humanity: in the clash over considerateness to servants, over Nance Mockridge in the yard, over dialect. Equally they are such as to advance the destruction of what he seeks with all his energies to preserve: old Casterbridge, his livelihood, his worth. He is humanly offensive in these pages, and he offends against the tongue of his own people. He is not simply, in himself, old Casterbridge; his pretensions are to lift himself, through his possessions and dominations, 'above' it. He takes some of his cues for estimating its ways from a dimly-perceived world outside it; a world, he obscurely knows, that holds the controlling power securely in its grasp, and out of his.

It seems to be a strategy for preserving all the elements of change in due relation, that sets Elizabeth-Jane's devotion to the dead mother alongside her studies. The devotion comes of the new loneliness, and the dissatisfaction with the style of life imposed upon her. She takes on, perhaps, something of Susan Henchard's aura: 'a dumb, deep-feeling great-eyed creature', a figure of 'patient fortitude'. It is winter, and on 'days of firmamental exhaustion which followed angry south-westerly tempests—when, if the sun shone, the air was like velvet—' she makes periodic visits to the burial place, with the most ancient past about it. I think it among the finest touches of the novel that the first encounter with Lucetta, the invader, the stranger, should be in that place and at that time.

[1] This is not a sentimentalist's jotting; it may be verified in (for instance) Haggard's *Rural England*, Hardy's own *Dorsetshire Labourer*, and the writings of Jefferies. Giles Winterborne's chivalry to Grace at the climax of *The Woodlanders* depends upon it.

THE INVADER

There at the grave, seeking the same figure of the dead countrywoman, is the ballad Lady, beautifully dressed, elegantly poised, the Invader. The costume and deportment work their own spell, in the setting of this story. Significantly, when Elizabeth-Jane returns to her father she slips into her mother's dialect. I call this Lady the Invader, having in mind the pattern common to Hardy's best imaginative fiction. Strong-natured country workers of deep local commitment are brought into relation with figures from outside the rural world. The contact occasions a feeling of menace; and as the landscape, the agriculture, the work, and the past, make themselves felt more strongly, the story assumes some form of conflict, and the invasion wreaks its havoc. Each novel makes a different life and movement from this cell, and it's a mistake to stereotype the formulation. In that spirit I used to identify Farfrae as the Invader, but I can no longer read *The Mayor* in that way. Farfrae comes from outside, but he joins; he is *for* the agricultural community, not a disrupter; he holds a hope of renovation in his skills and intelligence; created perhaps out of Hardy's truthful acknowledgement of local inadequacies.

But the force of Lucetta's invasion cannot be mistaken. There have been hints of a theme centred on 'rising in the world' on one side; and a theme centred on 'education' and 'insight' on the other. They seem alternative ways forward, or a way and a false attraction. These hints now gather insistence. When the Lady acquires the Hall, the idea of the Leisure Class imposes its terms unmistakably. Here is the end proposed by Henchard's meaner social aspirations: to transcend the menace to local agricultural life by ceding to the values of the propertied groups of the metropolis. As Alec d'Urberville and the Chase in *Tess*, so this Hall and this Lady: 'Blood built it, wealth enjoys it.' Some of its rooms overlook the market, and the Casterbridge market itself may seem changed when looked at through those windows.

The story develops in such a way as to bring Elizabeth-Jane and Henchard and Farfrae in turn into personal relationship with inherited wealth and the metropolitan manner. Elizabeth's relation makes its formal start in the graveyard where her mother lies, and at the back of the wall is 'a cornyard with its granary and barns'. But it cannot be ordinary relationship; the prose reflects the magic visitant, the agent of disturbance. 'Here in a churchyard old as civilization, in the worst of weathers, was a strange woman of curious fascinations never seen elsewhere: there might be some devilry about her presence.' [1] While the two make their compact the air is threaded with voices; 'such words as "sacks" "quarters" "threshing" "tailing" "next Saturday's market" ' come floating over the wall 'on the wind and raindrops'. The two worlds connect.

The Elizabeth-Jane who chooses to serve Lucetta is the daughter who will not be possessed, will not live out a rôle as part of Henchard's assets. Yet at this moment Henchard's uprightness, his faithfulness to the habits enjoined by the firm provincial moral code, remind us firmly who (at heart) he is. Even Susan's letter seemed to him no more than he deserved. His sense of obligation and responsibility is strong. But the absorption in market struggles against stronger forces dictates the terms in which human obligation speaks. When Susan returned to Casterbridge he had not only made the equivocal gesture of buying her back; another cash transaction to express responsibility had bought off the woman-in-the-past whom he had wronged, Lucetta. Now he discharges his obligations to Elizabeth-Jane in the same honourable and financial way. 'Honour' is the word here; Henchard honours debts, rather than fulfils responsibilities.

Henchard and Farfrae in turn fall under Lucetta's spell. She is not part of the strength of the novel, but the reserve of Hardy's portrait, the distance at which he keeps her, serve him well; and he is scrupulous and resourceful where her rôle in the story most nearly touches his deeper themes. Her arrogance about Susan in the first letter to Henchard is such a point. The analysis of Henchard's emotional veerings is another: 'By an almost mechanical transfer the sentiments which had run to waste since his estrangement from Elizabeth-Jane and Donald Farfrae gathered around Lucetta before they had grown dry.' He still seeks an extension of domain; yet he desires also to right a wrong, to hold faith with his code; obscurely, he also aspires to reserves of power through her, financial and social. It is a Lucetta 'sublimed into a lady of means' who casts the spell. But most admirable of all, in what concerns Lucetta, is the energetic finesse with which (in the scenes of Elizabeth-Jane's coming to the Hall, and the suitors following) Hardy establishes the leisured nullity of a false style of life.

The elegant boudoir overlooking the market square is a small triumph. Trivial prettinesses: absurd reclining postures: cushioned ease: the 'card

[1] The remarkable short story, *The Fiddler of the Reels*, makes the most vivid parable of all, touching such encounters.

tricks I have learned, to kill time'—all non-committally listed. The two ladies look out like *voyeurs* upon the market scene below. Its business continually occupies the prose and sets off the lethargy within doors. But this window confers distortions. Men are 'like trees walking' (for these *voyeurs* are nearly blind) and the place has the aspect of an Exchange. Ruffled cheque books regulate large bank balances. 'Gibbous human shapes' represent 'ready money'. It is an oblique etching of the economic face of modern times, and Henchard's fall is latent in those terms. Then the vision clears, as it were. We see the market of old Casterbridge again —the apple trees brought in by orchard men with the country clay on their boots.

DOUBLE STRANDS

Farfrae appears now in 'genteel cloth leggings with white buttons'. He has dressed his part in the new society, and the accidental encounter, not with Elizabeth-Jane but with Lucetta, seems the more fitting. Outside, the community is festive again: it is Fair Day. Their eyes go naturally to 'the busy scene'; but she 'looks at a picture, merely'. 'Your numerous fairs and markets keep me interested. How many things I think of while I watch from here.' She has no 'point of junction' with it all. He has. But just as earlier her gaze fastened grotesques with cheque books, now her company elicits primarily the financial astuteness that is making him master of the new Casterbridge market. 'A man must live where his money is made.' He is again the migrant, the market has drawn him with a kind of compulsion. His candid declaration is a submission to its terms: accumulation of stock, and finance-strategy: not to fulfil a necessary rôle in trade; not to connect Casterbridge with the agriculture of its country-side; but for its own sake, or for further reserves of financial power. And his declaration makes an image of that vaster process to which Caster-bridge itself must in time submit. Farfrae believes himself to be coming to terms with it by moderate astuteness.

'Yet I've done very well this year. O yes. You see that man with the drab kerseymere coat? I bought largely of him in the autumn when wheat was down, and then afterwards when it rose a little I sold off all I had! It brought only a small profit to me; while the farmers kept theirs, expecting higher figures—yes, though the rats were gnawing the ricks hollow. Just when I sold the markets went lower, and I bought up the corn of those who had been holding back at less price

c

than my first purchases. And then,' cried Farfrae impetuously, his face alight, 'I sold it a few weeks after, when it happened to go up again! And so, by contenting mysel' with small profits frequently repeated, I soon made five hundred pounds—yes!—(bringing down his hand upon the table, and quite forgetting where he was)—while the others by keeping theirs in hand made nothing at all!'

The technique extends the traditional wariness of farming communities and reaches out towards the idea of finance corporations. And this *declaratio fidei* is made to Lucetta, while Hardy observes the presence of 'double strands in Farfrae's thread of life', the man and the merchant not fully mingled.

The presence of the man declares itself when their attention returns to the market fair outside, its variety and colour and business, and they see the old unwanted shepherd standing aside in his 'stillness', an object of barter. The moment is lifted from one of the finest pages of Hardy's sociological essay, *The Dorsetshire Labourer*, a page concerned with migratory labour, the collapse of local social groups, and the poignant lot of the old under the new dispensation. In this paragraph of the novel, the figure of the shepherd in the human drama assumes a quiet symbolic stature; a prevision of the Henchard-to-be; a living instance of what the new market techniques and values are doing and costing. Though Farfrae has just been exulting in those techniques as if they were a game of skill, his manly self is touched by their consequences (and a flood of real but ignorant sentiment issues from Lucetta too). So he acts to preserve a family and enable a marriage; but he sees his act also as a feasible mercantile arrangement. 'I want a young carter; and perhaps I'll take the old man too—yes; he'll not be very expensive, and doubtless he will answer my purpose somehow.' The power that enables the generosity is the same power that has helped precipitate the need for it— a familiar image of the way benevolence works. It has its place within the strategy of commerce. But it is humane none the less. A 'bargain was struck', yet a purity of motive obtains which is at least an advance upon the barter of a while before.

The prolonged farewells between the two support the feeling (perhaps the strongest implicit feeling of the scene) that the milieu of leisured grace, the signs of affluence unmixed with trade, are enticing Farfrae. Then Lucetta, whose paid companion Elizabeth-Jane already is, starts using the girl as a ploy, manipulating her relationships. We recognize in a language the novel has made familiar by now, the market technique: the mechanical use of people to further deals and negotiations. The market in its various rôles continues to attract attention from page to page as the romantic union develops. A fine paragraph in XXIV, for instance, watches the farmers negotiate bulk and power under broad and threading sunlight and then (by firelight) watches the little people, vulnerable in a market controlled by the 'pounds' of 'the moneyed class', buying and selling on a miniature scale under lamplight. Always there is the business and flurry, beneath the window, of people active in the town's real livelihood.

METROPOLIS AND MARKET

But indeed chapter XXIV of which that paragraph is a part has a richness all its own. It is the chapter of the new dresses from London and the new machine from the north, set (not accidentally) side by side. There is a covert affiliation between them; the world that wears the one needs the other. The prose of the dress scene coruscates jauntily—a touch sardonic where dresses supersede personality. The two implied ladies lie out there upon the bed: 'You are that person (pointing to one of the arrangements), or you are *that* totally different person (pointing to the other), for the whole of the coming spring.' Lucetta, it's decided, will be the cherry-coloured person. And immediately after that bright artifice comes real brightness—sunlight falling flat upon other houses and pouring reflected brightness into the ladies' room; and 'circling irradiations' as the new machine arrives in the market place. Violent sallies of colour and shape suggest how the horse-drill afflicts local vision. Farmers crowd round, women draw near, children creep under and into it. To the lady of leisure it seems 'a sort of agricultural piano'. The sequence is masterly. Farfrae appears as its promoter, 'though not a farmer, closely leagued with farming operations'. The cherry-coloured person (accompanied by an Elizabeth-Jane who has 'pitch-forked on her bonnet and shawl') advances into the crowd, and seems to be the one appropriate possessor—'because she alone rivalled it in colour'. The mocking, uncomprehending Henchard stands by deriding: and then—superb climax—the gay sound of the Scots folk song from inside the machine, a frisky yet touching invention of Hardy's unique kind.[1] There is a severer note about mechanical advance at Flintcomb Ash in *Tess*; here the provincial recoil

[1] Consider, to match this, the poignant narrative image that culminates *The Son's Veto*, a characteristic short story of 1891.

from an absurd intrusion seems an element in a wider geniality. Farfrae can explain and support the new technique, and Elizabeth-Jane's phrase about 'the romance of the sower' distances and sets aside the old ways. But no certitudes accompany the new. Things change, and—' "Ay, ay . . . it must be so!" Donald admitted, his gaze fixing itself upon a blank point far away. But the machines are already very common in the East and North of England.' The process cannot be arrested, nor ought it to be.

The chapter's art is still unfinished. I am thinking less of Lucetta's confession to Elizabeth-Jane than of those painful questions at the end. We return to the lady of the London fashions. Her questions turn upon change and process as these affect the marketable worth of cultivated beauty. 'How do I appear to people?' The country girl's answers are quiet and grim. A whole circuit of meanings is completed by them. Throughout, the presence of 'Susan Henchard's daughter', a sensitive consciousness poised between the worlds, both social (now) and economic, seems to verify what passes; and in the next chapter too. Watching with her, what we see, we see.

TRANSITION

Farfrae's passion for Lucetta is called the unforced passion of youth, Henchard's 'the artificially stimulated coveting of age'. The judgements ring true, yet one leans to indulgence and the other to severity—a counter-balancing, perhaps, of the way the broad flow of the story might take us, unregardful. The tension between the two reaches its extreme as they collide, suitors of the propertied lady. The easy unison between the inner movement of the fable and the superficial matter of the plot intensifies the pressure we feel through such a scene as that between Henchard and Lucetta. The fusion between the rôle in saga and the human psychology of the moment enables a natural but pregnant dialogue. 'He's hot-tempered and stern. . . . I won't be a slave to the past.' The stuff of Victorian magazine fiction is serving imagination all right, and serving the deep movements of the whole novel. 'His voice slowly fell; he was conscious that in this room his accents and manner wore a roughness not observable in the street. He looked about the room at the novel hangings and ingenious furniture with which she had surrounded herself.' In this milieu Henchard loses his mastery, he becomes (it's Hardy's word) 'deferential'. The forty years between the Now of the story and the Now of its writing haunt the interchange that follows. Lucetta's 'fifty years more of civilization' have made their impact.

When she turns from him, 'a yellow flood of reflected sunlight filled the room for a few instants. It was produced by the passing of a load of newly trussed hay from the country, in a wagon marked with Farfrae's name. Beside it rode Farfrae himself on horseback.' Unseen by Henchard, Lucetta's face warms with consciousness of her lover risen 'like an apparition'. Sunlight has continually brightened the commerce of the market, threaded its way into all parts of the mosaic of Casterbridge, the real author and provider of the farming resources. This vision of reflected sunlit hay inside the room and the young triumphant agricultural merchant whose name the wagon bears riding beside it, confirms the feeling that the transition between the two men is a transition of agricultural potential. The chapter (and what for convenience I am treating as the first movement of the novel) ends on a note of bewildered pain, felt in the most alert consciousness—Elizabeth-Jane's. Her experience has not only been one of disappointments, but also of substitutions, renewals; and that experience is central to *The Mayor*.

3. *A Pause for Stock-taking*

What kind of novel?

POSSIBLE APPROACHES

This is a good place to break off, and make a few suggestions about the kind of novel *The Mayor* by now reveals itself to be. To take Hardy's novel for what it really is, and not to mistake it for a go at some other thing, both quickens admiration and sets certain limits to it. No very deep study is needed to discern several clear kinds of framework. The first reading of all—for many—yields the unrepeatable spell of a born story-teller (what Hardy felt George Eliot failed to be). 'We novelists are all Ancient Mariners,' he claimed: it is his simple but strong conviction about the outside of his art. And in one aspect, the narrative art subsequently continues to hold us—by the clear, firm compassion that animates it. Then there is the skill with which a variety of plot-material is woven together—really imaginative skill at times, as when Newson reappears for the first time in Peter's Finger. There is the severe, formal disposition of the parts within the architecture of a parabola, as one looks at the shape of the novel as a whole. I say little of these things; they are there to be found, they are good to find, and once found they yield nothing more than themselves. Equally, such flaws as the excessive variety of small incident and the evident 'to-be-continued' endings to section after section, are easy to find, and do no more to damage the real character of the novel than the formal excellences to sustain it. We do not read it as a magazine serial now. Some find the analogies between *The Mayor* and Greek drama interesting; and there is enough about the character and the fall of Henchard, and the 'conduct of the action', to bear out the known fact of Hardy's sympathetic studies in that field. But nothing (I think) that goes on illuminating, when one has taken note of it. So I have not much to say of the lonely, self-willed Promethean figure who looms so large in our first encounter with *The Mayor*; who blindly brings about his own destruction. This is a structure adumbrated, not a vision realized; there is little imaginative solidity to it.

Nor does study of the novel, in my experience, deepen or increase our appreciation of the personalities there. I have read that Henchard represents a subtle intuitive projection of 'the great 19th century myth of the isolated, damned and self-destructive individualist', a pre-Freudian exploration of the pathology of self-punishment.[1] But this is not at all the experience of reading Hardy's novel itself; such hints as we do find pointing in the psychological direction seem (once found) to dry up, to take us no further. Guerard's is a different novel about Henchard, not the one Hardy created. Hardy's psychology has the essential truth and penetration of provincial wisdom, wide reading, tradition; but not creative insight into the human spirit. So we need still to refer the question back: why this sketch (that's what we have) of the lonely Promethean figure blindly stumbling to his own defeat, taken that way by his own will-power? What pressures are at work? Isn't the figure we meet in the pages of the novel rather legendary than psychological?

What, then, of *The Mayor's* seasonal cycle, its hints of old rites such as stand behind saga and ancient drama alike? Does Hardy's imagination move with an anthropological tide? (His studies in religion and folklore had taken his mind in this direction.) Giles Winterborne appears more than once in *The Woodlanders* as if in a work of imaginative anthropology; there, and perhaps here, we feel Hardy seeking a valid imagery for permanence in nature, and indestructible worth. If we take our cue

---

[1] *Thomas Hardy: The Novels & Stories* by A. J. Guerard, pp. 146–52.

from the novel's title, recall Hardy's instinctive feeling for folklore and custom, and if (for instance) we look up the ballad of *John Barleycorn*,[1] we may find touch with a more distinct source of our continuing pleasure. The characteristic rite of continuity and renovation in agriculture, of seasonal change, is after all the slaying of priest or chief or king as Representative. Many of the rituals or games that survived longest in local life had reference to the combat between actors of the old and the new. Henchard appears (and this *is* his reality, surely) in three rôles, as mayor, as father, as corn-merchant; in each rôle we feel him supplanted. His very testament—I wonder to myself whether some old ceremonial game may not lie behind that will, with its outcast's burial: a ceremonial substitute for the ritual of scattering the body's members. The mummers' plays, village festivity and children's ceremonial games, the old folk songs of sowing and reaping—these are perhaps bodied forth into fresh, contemporary life in the destruction of the old mayor and corn-merchant, his strife with the new, his loss of fatherhood, and his outcast's death.

I do not suggest that *The Mayor* gives us directly a profound re-enactment of seasonal myth.[2] It remains far too unmistakably a Victorian serial fiction for that. But I do believe that to tune to this wave-length is to become more responsive to the inner life, the uniqueness, of the novel. Unlike the bold parabolic architecture, the rather rhetorical analogies with Greek drama, unlike the hints of psychological depths, this resonance does enable us to take the feel of the book, to see what it is about, to appreciate its kind. The power of the story is a power to seem legendary, to suggest the scale of saga, and that power is most discernible where the movement of plot and character finds closest touch with the folklore behind—is animated by the deep convictions and acknowledgements that the folklore expresses. Or it may be discerned where the movement of plot and character finds touch with the farming realities of the contemporary scene, where the novelist himself found his deepest imaginative commitments. It is—seen under another, related light—a

---

[1] *Penguin Book of English Folksong*, p. 56.
[2] D. A. Dike, in 'A Modern Oedipus' (*Essays in Criticism*), II. 2, 1952, says much of interest of both the Greek and the anthropological patterns. I am glad of the corroboration his article offers; it is stimulating, and ought to be consulted. But I think he makes the novel too clear and easy. I cannot follow him in all the details of his analogies, nor feel that he has hit on the effective *life* in the novel with which the old rites may put us in touch.

balladist's art, this kind of story-telling; and it is characteristic of Hardy, the Hardy of such short stories as *The Fiddler* and *The Three Strangers*, and the novelist of the girl poised between the quiet devoted soldier and the rakish sailor, of the seduced milkmaid, of fleeing lovers drowned in a weir amid storm and darkness, of the dashing soldier in scarlet and the patient lover of a lady above his station. He was a ballad-singer's son, nurtured in that tradition, and in a community that delighted to preserve it. His irony, then, is not subtle or philosophical; it is the stiffening sombre irony of remembered country tales, and of traditional ballads.[1]

These, I think, are the narrative forces at work, and part of Hardy's triumph lies in his assimilation into that bold, heroic and ironic mode, of the paraphernalia of Victorian magazine serials. The detail and topic of his plot-material take their life from the gravity and force of the under-lying saga, from the ballad rhythm; and the firm relationship of these to the themes the novel explores, communicates vitality to the outer parts, the turretry—even to the trivia of coincidence, the lightweight anecdote, the bits of 'French Romance', the passages in learned, pontifical or patronizing style. We need not deceive ourselves about the relative nullity of these in themselves. Least of all about the pretentious phrases and the passages of classical or biblical allusion, the self-conscious similes. They ring false, they seem to have been put in to make the prose resonate. We need not be deceived, either, about the novelist's tendency to go on about people and situations, rhetorically, from outside, without really advancing understanding beyond the humdrum level. Nor about the egregious symbolism of such things as the leering chipped mask boding ill from Lucetta's house (part of the trappings of later balladry) —things one skips on past, after a first reading. Nor can we miss for long a lack of interest (at the deep, creative level) in other human selves. When, out of tenderness, Hardy most desires to make the private heart communica-tive (as with Elizabeth-Jane at her mother's death) we feel *his* tenderness, *his* reflections, not the reality of the girl.

What he does take creative delight in is the quality of human com-munity, of reciprocal livelihood. The talk of the workmen and women of Casterbridge is stylized, but it communicates appreciation, it has its dignity as well as energy, it reflects a sense of the worthiness of lives so lived. It spares dialect but is thick with usage and custom, village relation-ships and history, methods of agriculture and commerce. When—as

[1] See my *Thomas Hardy*, pp. 108–12. Henchard appears reading ballads, and the moment is recalled as he goes from Casterbridge.

certainly happens—the commentary fuddles the report dramatically given, we must see the falsities in the light of Hardy's equivocal relation with a largely urban public (on account of whose susceptibilities he was recommended to withhold his first novel; he later destroyed it). Hardy no longer *belonged* to either the rural or the urban world; he was uncomfortably lodged between. Precisely his conviction of the value of the rural vision he has to convey (as well as his practical needs as a writer earning a livelihood) led him to try to write as a Literary Man. He does not really know or feel the interests and expectations of his readers. He has plenty of imaginative force but very little tact.[1] Of course, the curiously absurd quality of some scenes reflecting sophisticated life has another side to it. At first one feels simply that Lucetta in her boudoir (in this novel: there are parallels in others) is insecurely, falsely presented. Knowing the novel as a whole better one feels that very insecurity to be an important contribution to the whole. It becomes slowly clear that the absurdity one slips into receiving as Hardy's false step is an absurdity he finds *there*, in the milieu rendered.[2]

John Barleycorn amid the sun and rain; the countryman of older Dorset at that moment in history when his community and way of life as they have been for generations must suffer profound change (a change which, to the old, feels like defeat; a change which must, no doubt, include some irreparable human losses, whatever the gains): this, I take to be the subject, the double-subject, of Hardy's saga. In a moment I shall suggest that the heroic vitality communicated through Henchard comes of his bodying forth the plight of his community; and that novels of this kind had been written before. But before that it will be useful to look at the historical realities to which *The Mayor* bears witness.

FREE TRADE AND ENGLISH AGRICULTURE

'Free Trade has filled the towns and emptied our countryside; it has gorged the banks but left our rickyards bare.' That's the trenchant summary of Rider Haggard, in the final pages of *Rural England*, a documentary of fifty years to which Hardy himself contributed. And he found it impossible to take a favourable view of any aspect of Dorsetshire agriculture. The repeal of the Corn Laws was the 'moment' of *The Mayor*; the situation it precipitated forms the very substance of Hardy's important novels, their stories covering the forty-five years since, and ending with

[1] See my *Thomas Hardy*, pp. 118–20.
[2] Consider especially chapter XXXVII.

the contemporary *Jude*. But the rural collapse was an inevitable consequence of the chosen style of national growth; our vast prosperity depended upon Free Trade, and no other policy claimed serious attention.
The very structure of national trade hampered agricultural recovery.
Industrial growth required expanding exports of manufactured goods,
negotiable only for raw materials and cheap food. And behind the low
prices of imported foodstuffs lay a situation beyond our control. In
America particularly, railroad expansion over vast prairie lands, a new
abundance of steam transport at the ports, favourable climates, rich
virgin soil, and new labour-saving machinery, provided overwhelming
odds against our agriculture. The emigrating Farfrae was on to a good
thing. Ought he to have stayed? We had no agricultural leaders. Our
powerful figures were Henchards. Those who cared, those who farmed,
felt powerless—felt the impotence, in fact, of the characteristic Hardy
protagonist.

In 1846 Disraeli prophesied that Free Trade in Corn must ruin our
agriculture. Two decades of apparent prosperity passed (Farfrae's
decades). Our farming developed; wars abroad conspired to divert
foreign foodstuffs from our shores. Agricultural technology improved,
seasons were favourable, prices remained stable and fairly high, live-
stock breeding prospered. Rents and profits rose, but the labourers'
wages didn't; during winter the family often depended upon the easily-
exploited labour of wife and children. Meanwhile railroads brought the
towns nearer to the countryman, and a primary education designed for
the civic world spread. Flourishing industry, higher wages, the variety of
life and amenity, lured countrymen to the towns, and the exodus of
labourers began. The formation of an Agricultural Union could not
halt the drift, only plan it more sensitively. In the seventies the era of
apparent prosperity ended. Home produce couldn't compete with imports. Prices dropped. Farmers and landlords were gripped by uncertainty
and wages fell. A long struggle with the Union ended in defeat for
organized labour and the further spread of despondency, movement to
the towns, or emigration. The agricultural communities lacked any
manifest form of corporate strength, and the union movement weakened
further through internal dissension. In 1874, after another general fall in
wages, the storm broke. A trade depression, heavier imports of cheap
food, and a series of bad harvests from 1875 to 1879, an outbreak of
rinderpest in 1877, a loss of hundreds of thousands of sheep in 1878, an
annual cheapening of wheat—this was the tale of calamities. During those

years Hardy composed *Far from the Madding Crowd* and *The Return of the Native*.

During the seventies the area of wheat under cultivation fell by nearly a million acres, and sheep farming suffered even more extensively. The agricultural community numbered less than a million for the first time in centuries. And in 1883 the first period of catastrophe ended with an epidemic of foot-and-mouth disease which destroyed hundreds of thousands of cattle. The rich soil which bore heavy crops but cost more to cultivate was the first to be abandoned. There was a period of respite. But during 1886, when *The Mayor* appeared, agriculture was ruined a second time over. Imports extended; farmers could do no more, for their reserves were exhausted. So agriculture continued to decline; neither Parliament nor industry could help. Changes came over the farming class itself, and families with traditions of good husbandry who by thrift had survived the first depression, succumbed to the second. In 1891 Hardy roamed the Dorset countryside, dismayed by evidences of appalling disaster—crumbling buildings, decay and abandonment—and composed his most tragic fable of agricultural defeat, *Tess*.[1]

Locating his fable of *The Mayor*, then, in the period of the repeal of the Corn Laws, Hardy has chosen a passage of time when the old and the new are in tension, a time portending both division and calamity. His imaginative art takes its poignance from the knowledge of forty years since; knowledge of defeat for the old, of necessary adjustment, of profound social change. He has chosen a moment, too, in the history of finance capitalism when the possession of modest wealth still implies control, social responsibility, the opportunity of the entrepreneur. Hard work and energy suppose success. But there are forces felt to be at work which make small-scale control illusory, and responsibility too, and defy mere energy. The stockholder, the finance corporation, the boards of directors, are on the way. The corn-factor's rôle is no longer what it was, as we saw in Farfrae's manipulations (would he even have survived without them?) and the provision and dissemination of agricultural produce is at the mercy, increasingly, of the money-market. The patriarchal shepherd is a valedictory figure. And he, and the old-style corn-factor, are no longer relevant. Henchard cannot live on the terms the new order proposes. *The Mayor* takes us from a world of farmers and labourers winning sustenance (the world of *Far from the Madding Crowd*

---

[1] See the chapter on *Tess* in Arnold Kettle's *Introduction to the English Novel*.

and *The Return*) to a world of investment and profit, of wage-earners and merchants, of men who 'know nothing, sir, outside of eight shillings a week'. The centre (we see it shortly in Casterbridge itself) is no longer the farm but the bank.

Hardy's Henchard can rise to his feet and stand like a dark ruin; he can sway like a tree in wind: we feel no absurdity. His quality, the novel persuades, is not just personal. It is the calibre of a province, a style of life, expressed in a tremendous *vehemence* by an imaginative artist who feels a profound allegiance to that provincial society under strain, submitting to a process of alteration. To such imaginative artists there may come a stubborn prompting to assert with unmistakable force the spirit of the doomed clan; while at the same time recognizing the rightness of defeat and change so far as that is valid. To express all this, the legendary figure must needs bring about his defeat through those very qualities of energy and amazing vigour which represent the indomitable spirit of his group. And now there come to mind Henchard's real ancestors in our literature; and certain contemporary literary figures too, who may have particularly stimulated Hardy to create a hero to stand in the line of Redgauntlet and Fergus MacIvor; and a novel that, more than any others of the *Novels of Character and Environment* stands in the line of the *Waverley Novels*.

'THE MAYOR' AND 'REDGAUNTLET'

'Those who talk of Scott's "humanity" say too little by asserting too much; but this sense of what the community is, a feeling of and for community, is a major constituent, if it is not indeed the definitive distinction of what we apprehend too loosely as his "humanity".' Davie here points to something essential that brings Scott and Hardy together. It matters less to show parallel between Scott's imaginative preoccupation in the finest of the *Waverley* novels and Hardy's, than to identify a *kind* of novel, a way of giving fiction the ring of legend, common to both. It is misleading to say Either Or when asking if a novel projects human society or the individual heart, but it is not wrong to try to identify a quality of emphasis.

It was a phase of history that concerned Scott's imagination, and processes of change, resistance, and absorption that moved through his anxieties into tragic fables.[1] The new contemporary world, still absorb-

---

[1] I take support from an essay in *Literary Essays* by D. Daiches; two chapters of *The Hey-day of Sir Walter Scott* by D. Davie; and—in particular —from Edwin Muir's *Scott and Scotland*.

ing the Scottish provinces of the past, engaged a part of his sympathies and a completer acquiescence than Hardy conceded to his. But his sense of loss was passionate, and the novels explore and define it. He saw the movement of province into nation, clan into city, as an aspect of all historical process, good but grieving. The national, the industrial, the commercial, the legal, are aspects of more complex forms of social life, such as may extend personal life too: but the local and traditional forms disappear. It becomes a vital part of the imaginative labour to preserve a distinct record of customs, rituals, ways of speech: all the detail that makes up a style of life. (Hardy's footnotes, and the later prefaces, witness just this concern.) Such novels need, too, a mediating, pivotal consciousness: usually in Scott's fables a pilgrim or traveller in the places of stress, upon whom the old and the new, loss and gain, make their impact. Like Waverley, Elizabeth-Jane undergoes a long preparatory discipline for her rôle; her response is both sensitive and intelligent; her eventual commitment, in marriage to Farfrae, makes a replica of Waverley's. Hardy ends with a long testimony to her right to decide. Fergus MacIvor is the Michael Henchard there, and the mediating consciousness moves to and fro, clarifies issues, concedes what is due to honour and to valour on either side. Grief for the inevitable defeat of extreme and fiery clan loyalties matches deliberated connivance at the success of the new order. And part of the fineness of the art lies in this (as it does in *The Mayor*): that neither the old nor the new appear unspoiled. 'The novelist's achievement is in tilting neither way, but holding the balance scrupulously steady,' says Davie.

But *Redgauntlet* is the novel that has most to give and most to take, from being read alongside *The Mayor*. Its pivotal figure—like Elizabeth-Jane—does not know his parentage, and finds himself in a local world under strain, ignorant of who has shaped him and shaped it. On one side of him is Alan Fairford his friend and his father Saunders Fairford: a veritable embodiment of active, clear-sighted professional and legal life. Inevitably, where romantic ardour wills the restoration of its Province by rebellion, the Law must sharply focus the new establishment. It was also, historically, the basis of the thriving Edinburgh of the contemporary world.[1] Here is Farfrae (at first named Alan). On the other side a powerful romantic figuring of the old community's extreme term and prolonged vitality, a Henchard of the Jacobins. The same energy, flashing

---

[1] See Daiches, loc. cit.

eye, stern and gloomy pride and obduracy; the same incapacity to see how his own willed course of action invites defeat. Redgauntlet seems, says Muir, 'to incarnate Scott's conviction that Scotland was bound to lose its nationality, and that Scottish manners and character must unavoidably meet and dissolve into those of England'.

So the novelist in this tradition is driven to imagine his defeated community through the persistence of a priest-victim, a representative of its extreme term. He fights, conditioned by the very sources of his strength, 'tied down by the fetters of duty', 'limited by the regulations of honour'; and it is part of the legend of his defeat that he must meet that, against which his valour, and stern pride, and inflexibility, are powerless. What adversity nurtures, an act of grace, of magnanimity, of generosity, can out-manœuvre and throw down. For the magnanimity is an expression of the reserves of power latent behind it, the generosity also speaks of being able to *afford* generosity. The old virtues are flowing in the current of the new order: that is pain enough. They express its triumphant latent strength, partake in its strategy: that is unendurable. Redgauntlet's cry of despair finds an echo more than once as Henchard confronts a rival who can afford generosity, and who at the same time *is* generous. 'Nowhere else', says Muir, 'did Scott express so explicitly and vigorously his sense of the doom of the old heroic life.'

I do not know whether Fergus MacIvor and Redgauntlet and the Master of Ravenswood made part of the conscious imagining of Michael Henchard; it does not matter of what order of consciousness the debt. Hardy frequently re-read, and venerated, Scott; there is a reference to *The Bride of Lammermoor* in the text of *The Mayor* itself. But it is more important, I think, to discern the likeness of creative process, the likeness of imaginative response to social change. When the old order passes the community needs its heroic representative, its totem of primal vigour. But the local and provincial *are* passing, so the pride and obduracy of the chieftain must exceed his real and present function, must reflect an implicit recognition of impotence against odds. The community's extreme term must be felt conniving at defeat, its weapon glancing off the impregnable future and wounding only itself. So the process of defeat and change becomes a true saga, and a way of illuminating the loss and the gain, and enacting the difficulties of adjustment. In that context, the detail of a vanishing way of life matters.

There were other places for Hardy to find inspiration. There was the life and character of Anthony Trollope's father, detailed in Trollope's

Autobiography, that Hardy read the year before he wrote *The Mayor*. There was the masterful portrait of Mr. Tulliver in *The Mill on the Floss* of twenty years before. I cannot get it out of my mind that Hardy had this figure very much in his imagination in the later half of his novel. Tulliver too is bankrupted, and powerless, not least through obduracy and self-willed magnanimities; is impotent in a world of law and the property market. But to recollect the novel in which he figures is to be reminded of a creative power altogether more fecund and disturbing than Hardy's, in which the altering forms of social life and clan tradition (marvellously rendered though these are) subserve a profounder imagining of hearts and minds and motives and relationships, such as lies beyond Hardy's power. When Hardy strikes George Eliot's note of sympathetic moral commentary ('In such cases we attribute to an enemy a power of consistent action which we never find in ourselves or our friends; and forget that abortive efforts from want of heart are as possible to revenge as to generosity') we are surprised; and pleased. But the yield is less penetrating than hers.[1] On the other hand, Hardy's more confined interest enables a more memorable and powerful image of a community's transience. I have named George Eliot's novel because Hardy admired, and imperfectly understood, the author; and because a study of her novel alongside *The Mayor* (while it will not give and take as warmly as *Redgauntlet*) does clarify Hardy's art. If it also reminds us of Hardy's limits, in that too it does useful service.

Another novel to which a student of *The Mayor* ought to turn in the same spirit is *The Rainbow*—again, as much for illumination of what lies beyond Hardy as for insights bearing back upon Hardy (whom Lawrence admired). It's principally the figure of old Tom Brangwen who matters in this context; but Leavis's chapter on this novel in his book on Lawrence is called 'Lawrence and Tradition', and by keeping in touch with his analysis a reader is going to emerge with a more satisfying understanding both of the continuities and discontinuities of life between the older agricultural provinces and modern England. One more figure, one more novel, within this tradition, ought to be named: a community's veritable representative, created almost exactly while Henchard was: I mean Richard Jefferies's Iden, in *Amaryllis at the Fair*. This poignant valediction is there for the reading; but I cannot often persuade people to like it as much as I do myself. Coming freshly from it, a reader is less

[1] Cf. the passage beginning 'There is an outer chamber . . .' at the end of XLII.

than ever inclined to condone the failures of essential humanity into which the declining merchant of Casterbridge is betrayed.

I come back, finally, to the kind of saga-story that embodies the imaginative valediction, and exploration of change, in defeated provinces. It is grand and formal in outline. Its adhesions, its proliferations of plot and character, take such force as they have from the vigour of the sustaining saga. The elements of its fiction are like flotsam on subtle tideways; they exhibit the essential pulls and currents and movements of the deeper waters. They take the eye at the surface, but not to satisfy it: to trouble, and to reveal. We will turn back to the discussion of these deeper ebbings and flowings—the image has particular rightness for *Redgauntlet* or *The Mayor*.

4. 'The strong men shall bow themselves'

The merchant in Casterbridge market

A DOUBLE RIVALRY

The way possession (with full proprietary right) now of Elizabeth-Jane, now of Lucetta, becomes the focus of antagonism between the two men illuminates the currents that run through Casterbridge market into Casterbridge men and tend to make the acquisitive drives habitual. There is a speculative aspect too, to the personal relationships. Lucetta and her milieu cast an evident spell upon Farfrae; he is drawn to her; yet the later movement of the story leaves open the question, how much Scots canniness affected his choice of bride—the wedding is clandestine and precipitate. Certain of Henchard's hopes in Lucetta are speculative too; his forcing of her at the end of XXVII is manipulation at its grim extreme. He has speculated already in the attempt to release Elizabeth-Jane to Farfrae once his proprietary rights appeared unfounded. The attempt to exploit Lucetta's past occurs after the first warning sign of the return of the Furmity Woman, and his despicable conduct feels like a re-enactment of his earliest marketing of Susan. It gives the return of the woman to bear witness against him a disconcerting aptness, over and above the solemn irony. Now Henchard finds himself desiring to make use of marriage—marriage precisely as a public demonstration of his firm credit—to ease his financial straits. Yet the conscious purposes seem geared still to the older tradition. Honourable confusions embarrass his dealings with the terrified Lucetta when he discovers the clandestine marriage (she has been left vulnerable because Farfrae, even at such a time, cannot neglect a call of business). Her offer to buy him off—so tempting in this financial crisis—he repudiates indignantly by reference to the old code, to Redgauntlet's constraining honour, as it were. On the other hand the old code itself assumes a dubious public quality in Casterbridge now, and as the novel advances. Repute, sobriety, thrift take on the aspect of business assets rather than ethical ones. And the public valuations are suspect: 'market quotations' mislead. Casterbridge supposes Lucetta wealthy and high-born and pure, and Farfrae accepts the valuation. It is ignorant of its mayor's real past: a Furmity Woman's gossip in Mixen Lane can disturb the stock market—'she knew a thing or two about their great local man, if she chose to tell it'.[1] It is part of Henchard's older adherence to open dealing, that he should have disclosed that past freely, as he did, to Farfrae.

Henchard speculates in nature, too, when he stakes his reserves on a poor harvest. He too, now, uses his rôle as corn factor as a means to financial manipulation, and succumbs to the new market ethics Farfrae boyishly vaunted to Lucetta. His pride and vigour part embrace, part resist the new techniques. He wills the defeat of his rival in open economic strife, but 'by fair competition . . . as hard, keen and unflinching as fair . . . I've capital, mind ye, and I can do it'. But Jopp's rôle is subtle; a man who comes 'after dark, feeling his way through the hay and straw to the office where Henchard sat in solitude awaiting him'. He is at once the magazine villain who happens to know about the Jersey mésalliance; and the down-and-out worker, sitting vindictively loose to the employer who once arrogantly and unjustly dismissed him; and by envy of the brilliant new merchant who displaced him, sitting loose to the older moral code. Seen in saga terms he is the victim of the inhumane and irrational element of both the old Casterbridge and the new: the representative of Mixen Lane. Now he becomes the honourable merchant's ally.

At this moment of Henchard's stern determination Hardy chooses to indicate the forces operating on the wheat markets at the time of his tale, as though to throw the whole weight of agricultural change behind

[1] See D. A. Dike, loc. cit.

D

Henchard's decline. He emphasizes the intimate ties of feeling and instinct that bound the local communities to their land and to the seasonal rhythms. The commentary flows naturally into the ballad-stuff of the visit to the magician-forecaster, who draws his lore (half-fraud though he may be) from old tradition and folk-wisdom. Seasonal change conspires in the merchant's defeat; traditional lore misleads the man who would have used it for financial strategy. Efforts to mimic the new capitalist techniques are blind and ineffectual when dependent upon frail local ties. The residences of real power lie elsewhere. The defeat issues in two things: the false face assumed by the speculator covering up for awkward deals in the 'blaze of an August day'; and the crass inhumane treatment of Jopp—another re-enactment of dangers latent in the old-style ways of commerce: the arbitrary power of the employer. Between, giving a powerful lurch to the movement of the fable, comes the gloomy interview in the partners' room at the Bank. Henchard's property and produce become the possession of his bankers, though they continue to 'stand in his name': a momentous transaction. The understructure of the market reveals itself suddenly; asserts command; withdraws.[1]

THE COUNTRY STABILITY

But there is no more than a shadow cast upon the agricultural milieu itself by the new commerce. The sequence of chapters that leads to the revelation in the courthouse and Lucetta's clandestine marriage (XXVII–XXX) begins with the very feel of harvest-tide. The third paragraph of XXVII gives beautifully the personal movement and the eager perceptions of Hardy's most satisfying prose passages; its sharp images reach out into the interstices of the novel—rain and sunlight and energy. Even in this harvest setting we have Farfrae's canny moderation, striking just the right equipoise between competing possibilities, and bent upon the same objectives as Henchard's gamble intended. But the harvest dominates. It dominates first in the characteristic gay unsubtle invention of the two entangled wagons, Henchard's loaded to full height with hay, and tipped over when forced to yield right of way to Farfrae's wagon.[2] But Hardy continues with imaginative nicety to suggest the strengthening of

[1] See the chapter entitled 'The Bank' in Richard Jefferies's *Hodge and his Masters*.

[2] Compare the overturning of Mrs. Charmond's carriage amid the ruins of Winterborne's demolished house (*Woodlanders* XXVI), or the accident to Tess's wagon—and Kettle's note on it, loc. cit.

Farfrae's position by weaving his lover's walk with Lucetta into the scene of moonlight harvesting. 'Nearly the whole town had come into the field,' for the Durnover farming part of the community is supported by all those whose well-being is bound up with theirs. The louring Henchard who follows the lovers hears their intimate colloquy, and hears the festive gaiety of the harvesters, 'standing among the stubble' where 'the "stitches" or shocks rose like tents about the yellow expanse, those in the distance being lost in the moonlit haze'. He lodges there, related to the lovers and to the community by many threads; alone, amid the stubble. No less tender and subtle is the moment when Farfrae moves among the workers and Lucetta 'when they drew near the workpeople' withdraws home, while Henchard joins the 'activity, where the sheaves were being handed, a dozen a minute, upon the carts and waggons which carried them away'. The episode of the terror from the bull, and Henchard's strength and chivalry then, seems poor matter compared with this: but the balancing of the scales continues; Farfrae shows an equal delicacy.[1]

In two particulars the Elizabeth-Jane who listens to Lucetta's final disclosure calls us back to the earlier society. She becomes 'Susan Henchard's daughter' again; and she gives her absolute loyalty to the narrow rural pieties regarding the marriage bond: romantic love must yield to traditional 'honour'. So, leaving the house which she thinks of as the house her erstwhile suitor is to come to as master, the faithful lover of a man above her station (the ballad figure) withdraws.[2] She arrays herself in a plain dress, seeks modest lodging, and chooses a life of quiet labour and study, netting and reading. Meanwhile the social discredit that follows the disclosure in the courthouse becomes a financial liability; reputation

[1] The episode does touch upon the sensation of bewildered and frightened lost-ness of the urban invader in the natural world, superbly imaged when Mrs. Charmond and Grace are lost in Hintock woods in *The Woodlanders*. A first draft perhaps? Chapter XXIX is an example of the multiplication of incidents to fill a serial instalment, that Hardy himself regretted. A reader can easily find others. The wonder is that so much of this proliferation is made to serve the central inspiration so well.

[2] Not only does the girl here prefigure Marty, the rejected of Giles Winterborne; the episode of Farfrae's choice reproduces tacitly an important and recurrent Hardy image—to wed the country girl or the sophisticated lady? Cf. *Under the Greenwood Tree* and *The Woodlanders*, and (with reversed rôles) *Far from the Madding Crowd*.

can no longer sustain an illusion of 'credit'; Henchard's stock falls. Hardy quietly brings together the two interlocking terms: 'He passed the ridge of prosperity and honour.' Honour as public asset is gone. There remains the old honour, the good repute and sense of authority derived from a vital rôle in the community's livelihood; source of the 'blazing regard' now turned downward. Henchard seeks to uphold that honour still when financial defeat is total. It's 'the heavy failure of a debtor whom he had trusted generously' that finally overthrows his 'tottering credit'; and even the marketing of bad grain appears to result from implicit trust in his workmen. The same note of scrupulous honour sounds in the valid accounts at bankruptcy, the good intent to meet all debts and obligations; the special act of generosity to a small creditor in hard straits. In all this, as in his blundering in too subtle a world, Henchard recalls the warm, honourable, foolish Tulliver. Public talk is kinder to the underdog than to the top dog and remembers the energy which was Henchard's chief asset. A representative both of earlier farming and earlier capitalism, 'he had used his one talent of energy to create a position of affluence out of absolutely nothing'.

He withdraws to Jopp's cottage: the old-time employer and the rebellious worker come together. But it is also a withdrawal from the modern Casterbridge to the ancient, rural Casterbridge.

> Trees which seemed old enough to have been planted by the friars still stood around, and the back hatch of the original mill yet formed a cascade which had raised its terrific roar for centuries. The cottage itself was built of old stones from the long dismantled Priory, scraps of tracery, moulded window-jambs, and arch-labels, being mixed in with the rubble of the walls.

Elizabeth-Jane discovers her father thus retreated, and immediately after discovers how precisely his rival has advanced through Henchard's fall. There has been a take-over bid: the current jargon is apt to this point in the saga. 'Mr. Farfrae have bought the concern, and all of we work-folk with it.' The inextricable relations of commerce and commonalty remain. 'Mr, Farfrae is master here?' Yes; and the wage is lower. But there are compensations, both in security, and in human dignity. 'Though 'tis a shilling a week less I'm the richer man.' The chapter ends with energetic images of renewed and thriving trade: grain, and trusses of hay, and creaking wimbles adjusted to scales and steelyards. There is perceptive ordering of resources here, and a more sensitive approach to human relations; negotiation through trade union is not far off, one feels, and Farfrae will do well at it.

The next chapter (XXXII) makes more of the generous instincts of Farfrae and his sensitive treatment of the fallen rival. But we are rightly put in mind of the generosity that defeats the intractable Redgauntlet. For here too we are made aware of generosity as an expression and instrument of superior strength, as well as of warm feeling.—It *is* warm, too; unforeseen; it breaks Henchard's guard; it leads to the re-establishment of personal relationships: first, in the corn-stores, then in the home with Elizabeth-Jane. He resumes his more fundamental, trained rôle: journeyman hay-trusser, he moves about the countryside with Casterbridge as his base. But he wears still the clothes of mastery and mayoralty, not the 'clean, suitable clothes, light and cheerful in hue; leggings yellow as marigolds, corduroys immaculate as new flax, and a neckerchief like a flower-garden' of the hay-trusser of an older time. What he wears now remembers a style of affluence and prestige; but has no relation to present Casterbridge.

THE DEFEATED COMPETITOR

The scene of Henchard's return to drink, and his commination of his rival, sustains the scale of saga while bringing a stronger, warmer quality of human feeling into the struggle. It matches itself to the larger rhythm of the novel by its aspect of music, festivity, the presence of the gathered community; and by the sense of sacrilege, of the perversion of old rites, that belongs to the climax. Henchard's altered rôle is defined by his settling, now, to The Three Mariners, the labourers' inn. The chapter begins with a fascinating sociologist's report, bearing particularly upon the force of custom in forging ties between men; and the drama that appears to grow imperceptibly out of the report is in Hardy's finest style. Henchard's voice moves with the rhythms of a powerful, regardless ego (one needs to hear a Dorset man utter the phrases) and the assumption of the heroic rôle, proud hater of the young successful upstart, is admirable. By taking the psalm, to Old Wiltshire, for his cursing he identifies his passion with the old usages of his people. The violent distortion notwithstanding, the psalm belongs to the community at its traditional worship. In a grim way—by Hardy's thread of deliberate irony—it is song for song; Farfrae's sophisticated folk-song of the distant north for the psalm and tune of the parish church. But for all the 'volcanic fires' of his nature, the figure who leaves the inn walks 'blankly, like a blind man'. And the words that ring in his mind, that he repeats still to himself, recoil upon him; they tell of change and forgetfulness.

Alongside the saga scale of that scene Hardy places a sharp grotesque vignette: Lucetta, the lady of leisure, walks in Farfrae's yards among the workmen, and Henchard—in that rôle—vents sarcasms upon her. 'We of the lower classes, ma'am' from one who had been her lover and equal denotes a ludicrous unreality in the changing class structures that depend upon new commerce; and her present rôle is as sharply specified by his allusion to 'gay leisure'. He means to wound, and does; within a page of 'a feeling of delicacy, which ever prompted Faifrae to avoid anything that might seem like triumphing over a fallen rval'. Lucetta takes care, now, 'not to come again among the hay and corn'. She would entice her husband to other places and milieux.[1] They are usually together (during these chapters) with curtains drawn and candles lit. He for his part, accepting the proposal to stand as mayor, is acceding to the lure of prestige, and Hardy deftly insinuates that into his acceptance. His attitude towards Elizabeth-Jane, the girl he had courted, is wounding in its turn, and made to feel the more so—at the start of XXXIV—by the beautiful invocation of the Casterbridge reality before their encounter, and the business of workfolk about the streets after it. And his impulse to set Henchard up on his own in a small seed shop: what a disconcerting mix-ture Hardy points to—of essential generosity; of self-defence; of the quieting of an uneasy conscience, guilty of indefinite wrongs; of the cultivation of public esteem. But this is a passage of strength in an area of poverty: the matter of XXXIV to XXXVI shows that stretching of invention to fill instalments already noticed. It's the least inspired part of the novel; even Hardy's visualizing power, and his concern with the mean-ing of the past, and his feeling for sunlight and rain, are stage-managed at times. The amphitheatre becomes imposing décor; Jopp metamorphoses into a melodramatic figure of evil, trebly involved in coincidence; and the prose offers such enormities as 'The sun was resting on the hill like a drop of blood on an eyelid.' Only the memory the amphitheatre scene brings back of Susan Henchard, the linking of the one ill-used woman with the other, releases for a short passage a more compassionate and genuine narrative.

But the royal visit is quite another matter. The acidity here issues from the centre of the novel's findings. An aura of pretension and absurdity

---

[1] See XXXIV, for instance.

surrounds the metropolitan centre; and that centre is felt inaugurating and sustaining irrelevant and deceptive locales of prestige. Real power, nationally and provincially, rests elsewhere; but this veneer is more comfortable. Hardy has all this in view. It's a new engineering work that the Royal Personage (Hardy's styling) is *en route* for. The Establishment is ostentatiously behind the processes of change; its representative himself zealously 'promotes designs for placing the art of farming on a more scientific footing'. Hence the invitation to Casterbridge. The tone of the commentary conceals irony not very far beneath a surface of accommodating respect. Among the essential objects of such Visits is the stir they create among the 'lower stratum' (the workmen in fact weigh impartially the attractions of this Spectacle with those of their Skimmity Ride). Farfrae, as 'the Mayor and a man of money, engrossed with affairs and ambitions, had lost in the eyes of the poorer inhabitants . . . the charm he had had as a penniless singer'. He is on Their side, now. 'Half an hour was not long,' we are told, '*but much might be done in it by a judicious grouping of incidents.*' Amid all the paraphernalia, Henchard, the representative old labourer, plays the parody-mayor with the parody-flag. So to the superb moment of the proffered handshake; the thrilled horror; the patronage; the hasty restoration of propriety. Hardy's prose is wickedly inscrutable. Certainly he does not convey a sense of real affront. 'The incident had occupied but a few moments, but it was necessarily witnessed by the Royal Personage, who, however, with practised tact, affected not to have noticed anything unusual. He alighted, the Mayor advanced, the address was read; the Illustrious Personage replied . . .' The two worlds, traditional and modern, have each their corny and their sinister side. For the traditional, there is the Skimmity Ride to come. 'As a wind-up to the Royal Visit . . .'

This sequence began with the stuff of legend—the commination at the Inn; it ends so, with the wrestling bout in the hay loft. And both scenes give a fine edge of personal feeling to the symbolic rivalry. We can recognize, before the drama itself, the signs of power: another invocation of Casterbridge, the 'nerve-knot of the surrounding countryside,' with the presence of sacks, horses, tools, work; then a delicate printing of light and growth in chestnut trees and drooping lime (with a half-hint of the prime Scot and the old worn man), and the play of warmth and sunlight on human features. A moment of song recalls earlier turning-points, and touches the spring of Henchard's deeper human instincts. The personal combat follows, the old man fighting with a self-imposed handicap because the old code matters more than victory. And in the event, the limit of Henchard's intent is to reassert virile potency; given the opportunity for mere destruction of life, a simple common bond quickly turns the issue. It's as though the old clan having demonstrated its strength, desires no more; withdraws; submits to the future acquiescently. At the same time, the encounter makes us feel brute strength to be at a loss beside delicacy. The process of change leans upon that, whatever more primitive reserves may still offer.

THE COMMUNITY OF THE DISCARDED

It is not the least of *The Mayor*'s subtler movements, that when Henchard resumes his labourer's rôle and strides in the terraces of defeat, Hardy's imagination occupies itself with the whole community of the defeated and the unwanted, the cast-offs of progress. Hardy may not achieve (in XXXII, where defeat sets in) an ideal sureness of understanding; he knows there is a force of repercussion at work, and he scarcely sees the justice in it. But his imagination really is working among the failures, the mistaken, those who have fought and lost in trade, those for whom suicide was a natural way out. If he fails in penetrating analysis of a society that produces, and casts off its useless produce so, still the dispositions of weight, the movement of the story, and the explicit tenderness towards the fallen and the helpless, connect together to make an observant, distressing and sombre report. Imagination, as often, gets beyond ordinary intelligence in marshalling the real facts. The picture of the three bridges and the third Inn, the indication of the third society in Casterbridge, complete a pattern that has hitherto remained too idyllic. The Mixen Lane of XXXVI is 'a mildewed leaf in the sturdy and flourishing Casterbridge plant': but its reciprocal relation with the town comes out in the succeeding image, and its complicity in the whole state of southern agriculture in the next page. Compassion is especially directed towards the village lifeholders of past days, now homeless and migrant. Not only *The Dorsetshire Labourer* (where Hardy argues that profound uncertainties of tenure have moral consequences; result in a more cynical view of the duties of life) but *The Woodlanders* and *Tess* show the fate of the migrant homeless, the loss of tenure, to be a vivid image for him of the essential distress and breakdown in Dorsetshire agriculture. If the sociological analysis on these pages is again a bit jocose, it is rare enough to have any such imaginative anxiety at all.

Inns have become, by the end of the novel, particular symbols of segregation. They used to exhibit clan characteristics; now they exhibit class distinctions. But there are covert ties between all three; there is that social *motion* shown us in the novel at large. The talk in Peter's Finger in XXXVI strikes me as one of the strongest passages anywhere in Hardy— one to turn to when the doubt is raised, whether the village talk in his novels isn't phoney and pseudo-Shakespearean. For all the verve and the appreciation of intrinsic human worth, the quality of life revealed is mean enough, and pitiful. The talk has its penetrations; Lucetta is named for 'the proud piece of silk and waxwork' that, in one aspect, she is. But the whole project of the skimmington ride, the envy and the cruelty animating it, indict old Casterbridge. Once it may have been a harsh way to uphold local pieties regarding marriage; it has anyway gone sour. There is nothing humanly worth preserving in such traditions as these. The ride is a grotesque parody of old games, and it expresses the vindictiveness bred in the hearts of the oppressed. Hardy's projection of it into his tale is finely timed. It salvages the weaker romantic stuff in his plot; it maliciously balances the Royal Visit; and it casts a grim shadow across Henchard's wrestling victory—mixes scurrility into that virility. The workmen who are not among the defeated and the rebels, have sensitivity enough left to want to save Farfrae from the pain of it. Then the scene unfolds in a masterly way. The distant noises reach Henchard's ear first while he labours under a sense of degradation, 'a confusion of rhythmical noises to which the streets added yet more confusion by encumbering them with echoes'. The sights and noises and movements of festive hate: the pain and distress of the women within doors: the swiftness with which a woman dies, and the game turns bitterly serious: Henchard's night wanderings in gloom—the sequence, and the judgement of weight and manner, fix and chasten our attention from page to page. The final paragraphs of XL fitly culminate it all. How sure is Hardy's touch when death comes; the prose (sensitive as ever to stirring and continuing vitality even at this hour) has the Dickensian quality of participation in the common order of life: but the experience is marshalled with a different dignity.

NEW ADJUSTMENTS

Hardy is quick to absorb the risen-from-the-dead Newson into a dramatic scene: and in the terms of balladry the bitter, deprived father in his fear, and the accuser, are real enough. But the deeper interest lies elsewhere: in the stirring of disinterested affection for the daughter no longer his in law or custody. 'Shorn one by one of all his other interests his life seemed to be centring on the personality of his step-daughter.' Is it because Casterbridge and the future are no longer tractable? Is it still, at bottom, because others desire her? How far is it a sense of human need, and how far a desire of reciprocal affection? How far an aspect of withdrawal from the tensions of Casterbridge? She goes from him 'up the hill in morning sunlight' with assurances of return. His affection is 'jealously' strong; his absurd lie to Newson manifestly prompted by the latent instinct of defiant possession. 'There would remain nobody for him to be proud of, nobody to fortify him': the use of relationship in a context of social forms remains still. And the lie retains 'a coveted treasure', his 'paternal regard' is heightened by a burning dread of rivalry. When Farfrae resumes his interest in Elizabeth-Jane too, the latent desire of sole ownership seems to prohibit still the insight which must discern prosperity and adjustment of demands in a match between the two.

Farfrae's recovery from loss and his pursuit of Elizabeth-Jane derive both from the 'insight, briskness and rapidity of his nature' and the demands of the Casterbridge market. XLII offers a last colourful glimpse of the town's rustic business, for groundwork to his courting. The girl he courts resumes her studies; he comes to her with the grain in his hair, but he comes with books. The union between them joins a thriving commerce to the search for deeper consciousness, for fuller comprehension, of the modern world. But these suggestions are quietly submissive to the natural flow of the story. The courted girl is her father's daughter, a roving man of no abode—her real father's; it seems almost a facet of her studies that she goes daily out along the Bournemouth road to catch glimpses of the distant sea.

Henchard has learnt a kind of love, it seems; but the values he has lived by, property rights and fair exchange, are waiting to exclude him. And he watches, bereft and powerless. His will is towards suicide, and the scene of his attempt (thwarted by miracle, after the style of some old village anecdote) defines his predicament. The narrative of it is compelling, grounded in local detail, time and place. And it prepares sombrely for the elegiac finale to the whole novel, when his actual death is mediated through a Casterbridge workman. 'The whole land ahead of him was as darkness itself; there was nothing to come, nothing to wait for.'

5. *Elegy for the Defeated*

lament.

The labourer in Weydon countryside

The last two chapters of *The Mayor* balance the first two. Except for Hardy's own reflective interventions, we are restored purely to the terms of saga. They are eloquent terms, for by now the testimony they bear is heavy with the novel's whole weight. The pervading sensation is twofold: it is of stoical defeat, and of elegiac regret. The final chapter is among the great heights in Hardy; but the author's meditations I habitually skip now—though I have to recognize a sombre and honest record being borne: this is how life goes. The tremors and distresses special to Wessex in its phase of ebbing hope are accommodated to the larger rhythm of human affairs.

When all vestige of rights in Elizabeth-Jane have gone, Henchard's affection seems purer than before; but this is at parting. Hardy seems here to hint at possibilities for life that Henchard, by commitment and by nature, hasn't been able to tap. As he makes his solitary journey out of Casterbridge, he assumes the full measure of the saga protagonist's rôle. Clothing has been important all along, because it has such detailed and varied and traditional relation to vocation and skill, to status and responsibility, to the interstices of social life. Hardy's use of it matches the alertness of a social investigator to the flair of a balladist. So here. Michael Henchard discards the clothes of gentility and mercantile prestige and becomes again the skilled Dorsetshire labourer: the representative figure the novel first envisaged.

> During the day he had bought a new tool-basket, cleaned up his old hay-knife and wimble, set himself up in fresh leggings, knee-naps and corduroys, and in other ways gone back to the working clothes of his young manhood. . . . He went secretly and alone.

He had left by the bridge of defeat, accompanied by Elizabeth-Jane only; the girl preparing her union with Farfrae; but still, to the end, the receiving spirit, the watcher of the novel. The vanishing figure yields a serene passage of diminishment, which is at the same time a transformation—the mere single human spirit becomes his Kind. 'She

59

watched his form diminish across the moor, the yellow rush-basket at his back moving up and down with each tread, and the creases behind his knees coming and going alternately till she could no longer see them.'

Hardy magnifies the accompaniment as he makes his journey, but the prose, if it rings loudly, is never out of key: 'I—Cain—go alone as I deserve—an outcast and a vagabond.' He sustains the rôle; and his stern subdual of anguish involves the shouldering of his basket. He cannot any longer (we are at XLIV) accept absorption into human societies. Implicitly we feel what the old folk rites behind the solitary going suggested: that his alienation, the completeness of his vanishing, and the wide areas which, dying, he visits, make obscurely for renewal. (Between the scenes of his loneliness Elizabeth-Jane and her real father and her lover are serenely united. But this seems only a momentary glow to deepen the essentially elegiac mood.) It is like the return of a man to his natural home. He lies down under a hay-rick, sleeps profoundly, and is wakened by 'the bright autumn sun shining into his eyes across the stubble'. Then once again, distant, the figure ceases to be Henchard, and becomes a labourer on the move, a rush-basket glimpsed between hedges, a flash of yellow among twigs. So he passes the hill of Weydon Fair, 'held for many generations', a hill 'now bare of human beings and almost aught beside'. At Weydon-Priors, briefly, the past and its pain lives again.

The image of Casterbridge as the inevitable centre for circuitous migrations is offered portentously (and much of the author's reflection is really disconcerting, however serious and compassionate) but it is perfectly just; Henchard knows no rival reality, he is of Casterbridge or nothing. That thoughts of Elizabeth-Jane should draw him there fits as well the movement of the general fable, as the broken heart of the man. And the movement of the fable goes beautifully. The hay-trusser works by highways connecting Casterbridge with the outer boroughs and the metropolis itself. His hay-knife 'crunches down among the sweet-smelling grassy stems'. The essential pathos dignifies the figure: so much vitality, so much potentiality, totally at a loss.

As in the momentary glow of reunion between daughter and father in Farfrae's house, so in the penultimate chapter, the elegiac feeling and the sense of defeat savour more poignantly by relation to the novel's last scene of festivity. The more so since the wedding celebrated in music and dance by so large a gathering is a commitment to change, to the new forces; a profound adjustment. The Henchard who is drawn to be present makes a last change of clothes. There is respect due to the wedding ceremonial; and is there not a special pathos in the impulsive choice of gift—natural life to become decoration? The later image of dead bird caged, out of its element, reflects in many ways into the novel at large; but the choice itself has its own sadness. Approaching the festivities he is again 'a lonely figure on the broad white highway'. There is the noise of music and gaiety; a pressure upon him of many people together, coming and going, up and down; extravagant lights: he feels out of element, social and spiritual element alike. The watcher in the outer kitchen presents an unforgettable image of the hopeless *voyeur*, debarred from song and soceity and beyond the vigour and partnership of dancing. The vision of zest there, of immoderate appetite for life, dismays and baffles him. The renewing processes hurt. He sees Farfrae and Elizabeth-Jane not so much dancing together as involved in the dance of a whole society, coming together now and again with delight, and parting; secure. He is indeed of heroic stature as he rises 'like a dark ruin', yet the mere human talk between step-father and daughter is very touching, and Henchard's last speech seems to me one of Hardy's greatest passages. His locked lips, and refusal of all excuse and explanation, is the last direct sight of him we have. The 'vice' clamps down upon so much capacity; the obdurate strength is still turned destructively upon itself. 'She saw him no more,' and the marriage festivities go on.

Henchard disappears, as it were, into the countryside. 'He had apparently sunk into the earth.' The living track his vanishing by 'a forking highway which skirted the north of Egdon heath'. Beyond Egdon—and it is like following some primeval figure into ancestral regions—the trackers 'were soon bowling across that ancient country whose surface had never been stirred to a finger's depth, save by the scratchings of rabbits, since brushed by the feet of the earliest tribes'. (Into such regions Tess, too, finally retreats.) Here are the Roman tumuli, 'dun and shagged'. But the trackers have to follow yet further into the past: to Anglebury, and a northern extension of Egdon. And there, Farfrae and his wife discover the workman, Whittle—himself coming upon the scene as a type of the predicament of the old order: 'his gait was shambling, his regard fixed in front of him as absolutely as if he wore blinkers; and in his hand he carried a few sticks'.

As for Whittle's narrative, the greatest elegy of them all, it seems to me beyond praise, a kind of art that is all Hardy's own.[1] Henchard's

[1] A more detailed study of this passage of the novel may be found in my *Thomas Hardy*, pp. 131-4.

stature and significance get their final definition through a workman's vision of him; they are verified so. Whittle's accompanying of Henchard out of Casterbridge and on his last journey reveals itself as a grace of reciprocal kindness: 'Ye were kind-like to mother . . . and I would fain be kind-like to you.' But Hardy's choice of this way to record Henchard's passing has the additional force of rendering it as social fact, received by a rougher cast of consciousness: not a drama for self-conscious pathos and the stirring of appropriate emotions. There is, indeed, in Whittle's narrative a dignified consciousness of responsibility for the time being —and a touch of pleasure in spinning the tale out; a buoyancy that raises despondency. It has the effect of making the bitter end remote, even while its details, particular or touching, verify the event. Its language reaches back through the texture of the novel: to the places in Caster-bridge, the changing relationships in the corn-merchant's yard. Like the art of *The Mayor* itself at its best, it is absorbed in the incidents themselves, in what happened: the signification can speak for itself. So the rude pride and authoritativeness of Henchard, even at the end, emerge unrelieved. And death is acknowledged and received without solemn emotion or fuss; and still in company; 'one of the neighbours have gone to get a man to measure him'.

All Hardy's art goes into imagining Henchard's death rather as a loss in community than as the extinction of an individual self. Farfrae is genteel and clumsy, confronting Whittle, and hearing; Elizabeth-Jane silent, and later stoical. And the workman runs for the piece of paper with some writing upon it; the paper through which, in a paradox, Henchard's vitality flows out. He is agricultural man, defeated: leaving no posterity; his one foster-child united to his young successor and the future. But his voice (it is a voice we hear, again) speaks the language of the older traditional sanctities, now fractured and discarded. The curt testament, with the social pieties of funeral still living in its authoritative phrases, is a self-annihilation; a repudiation; and yet a signing of the name to a last transaction, a deed of gift.

Further Reading

Novels

Waverley and *Redgauntlet*	Walter Scott
The Return of the Native, The Woodlanders and *Tess of the d'Urberilles*	Thomas Hardy
The Mill on the Floss	George Eliot
Amaryllis at the Fair	Richard Jefferies
The Rainbow	D. H. Lawrence

Changing Social Scene

Fiction and the Reading Public	Q. D. Leavis (Chatto and Windus)
Hodge and his Masters	Richard Jefferies (Faber and Faber)
The Dorsetshire Labourer (in *Longman's Magazine*, 1883)	Thomas Hardy (Longmans, Green)
Village Life and Labour	C. Hutchinson and F. Chapman (Cambridge U.P.)
Rural England	Rider Haggard (Longmans, Green)
Theory of the Leisure Class	Thorstein Veblen (Mentor Books)

Criticism

The Art of Thomas Hardy	Lionel Johnson (Bodley Head)
Thomas Hardy: Novels and Tales	A. Guerard (Oxford U.P.)
Thomas Hardy	Douglas Brown (Longmans, Green)

Criticism (*continued*)

Hardy: A Collection of Critical Essays	ed. A. Guerard (Spectrum Books)
Thomas Hardy	G. Wing (Oliver and Boyd)
Introduction to the English Novel	Arnold Kettle (Hutchinson)
'A Modern Oedipus' in *Essays in Criticism*, Vol. II no. 2	D. A. Dike (Oxford U.P.)
Scott and Scotland	Edwin Muir (Routledge)
Literary Essays	David Daiches (Oliver and Boyd)
The Hey-day of Sir Walter Scott	Donald Davie (Routledge)
D. H. Lawrence: Novelist	F. R. Leavis (Chatto and Windus)